A Short Introduction to

Understanding and
Supporting Children
and Young People
Who Self-Harm

Carol Fitzpatrick

A Short Introduction to
Understanding
and **Supporting**
Children and
Young People Who
Self-Harm

Jessica Kingsley *Publishers*
London and Philadelphia

First published in 2012
by Jessica Kingsley Publishers
116 Pentonville Road
London N1 9JB, UK
and
400 Market Street, Suite 400
Philadelphia, PA 19106, USA

www.jkp.com

Library of Congress Cataloging in Publication Data
A CIP catalog record for this book is available from the Library of Congress

British Library Cataloguing in Publication Data
A CIP catalogue record for this book is available from the British Library

ISBN 978 1 84905 281 8
eISBN 978 0 85700 584 7

CONTENTS

PREFACE

This book is written for those who care for and about young people who self-harm. Being a parent or carer of such a young person can be a terrifying and bewildering experience. Self-harm and suicidal behaviours are increasingly common in young people, but are often hidden problems. Parents and carers may know or suspect that something is wrong, but not know what. They often have a huge mixture of feelings – concern, guilt, helplessness, anger, but above all worry. Is there a risk of suicide? What is causing the self-harm? Does he need help? What help is available? How can I persuade my young person to go for help? Is it my fault?

Working as a child psychiatrist for many years with young people with self-harm and suicidal behaviour, and with their parents and carers, I have learned a great deal about the turmoil experienced by those in closest contact with these young people. I have also learned much about the value of the support provided by those parents and carers, and how this can be a most powerful asset in helping young people through their difficulties. This book attempts to share that experience and knowledge with the many people who come into contact with young people who self-harm, whether they are parents, relatives, teachers, youth workers, care staff, sports coaches, even staff in accident and emergency departments who are often the first professionals these young people meet. The book has a positive approach, combining practical advice with the most up-to-date research in the area of self-harm and suicidal behaviour in young people. The case reports are based on real-life situations, with details changed to ensure anonymity for the young people and their families.

I would like to thank all the young people, their parents, extended families, teachers and care staff, whose experiences have enriched this book. The book would never have been written without the support of wonderful colleagues in St Frances Clinic, the Children's University Hospital, Temple Street, Dublin, and at the Mater Child and Adolescent Mental Health Service in Dublin. Nor would it have been written without the support of my husband and grown-up children, who have taught me so much about family life. Thank you also to Deirdre Corrigan, who patiently read and re-read the book, and gave me wise advice.

Please note that I have adopted the use of alternate genders on a chapter by chapter basis to avoid the use of 'them', 'they', etc. This is an issue that affects both boys and girls.

I use the term 'young people' throughout the book to refer to both children and young people. Self-harm does occur in young children, but thankfully is much less common than in adolescents or young adults.

CHAPTER 1

WHAT IS SELF-HARM AND SUICIDAL BEHAVIOUR?

This chapter provides an introduction to and an outline of the whole book, acknowledging for readers how difficult and distressing it is to deal with the subject of self-harm and suicidal behaviour, while encouraging them to persist and to appreciate that their support can be an invaluable asset to the young people in their lives. It includes an overview of the different meanings of the term 'self-harm', what is known about the causes, who is at risk, and how mental health professionals assess young people who self-harm.

BECKY'S STORY

Becky, aged 14, has just been discharged from the hospital accident and emergency department. She was admitted there the previous night, having taken an overdose of about five paracetamol tablets following a row with her mum. She took the tablets, which she found in the bathroom, on impulse, and then got scared and told her sister what she had done. Her sister told her mum, who called an ambulance.

Becky had some blood tests in the hospital, and was told that the levels of paracetamol were not in the range which needed treatment. She was relieved, as she was frightened she had done serious harm to herself. She had to see a psychiatrist, who asked lots of questions, including one about why she had done it. Becky found that impossible to answer, she had not had time to think...she just did it. The psychiatrist also spoke with her parents, and now all three are on their way home.

Becky's parents, John and Angela, are distraught. This came 'out of the blue', although Becky had been going through a difficult time lately, struggling at school with her work, and she had fallen out with her best friend. There had been many rows with her over the previous week, mainly because of her sullen attitude and refusal to help at home. Her parents cannot understand why she took an overdose, and are terrified it will happen again. They were told that Becky would be referred to the local child and adolescent mental health service, and that they would get an appointment shortly, but they wonder what are they to do in the meantime? Where can they get support?

SANDY'S STORY

Liz is the mother of Sandy, aged 15. Liz has seen scratch marks and cuts on Sandy's left forearm several times over the previous few weeks, and she wonders how she could have got them. She has asked Sandy, who said she got them playing hockey in school, but Liz does not know whether to believe her – they don't look as if they could be the result of a hockey injury, and why would they keep appearing? She does not know what to do. She wonders if Sandy is alright, she used to be so easy to communicate with, but lately she has been spending hours in her room, and seems to have isolated herself from the family. When Liz asks Sandy if she is alright, Sandy answers angrily that she is 'fine', and tells her mother to 'stop wrecking my head'.

Continued on p.43.

JOHN'S STORY

John is 16. He lives with his dad since his parents separated last year. He also spends time with his mum. Relationships between his parents are difficult, and John finds this hard to deal with. John's teachers have noticed a big change in him in recent months. He has become more angry and withdrawn, is missing a lot of school, and seems to have lost interest in his friends and in his school work. A past pupil of the school died by suicide earlier in the year, and John's teachers are concerned because many things about John's behaviour remind them of that young man. They wonder how to help John.

While the situations above are very different, they have one thing in common – they all involve adults who are worried that young people in their care are at risk of harming themselves, or of attempting suicide. This is a devastating worry, particularly for parents, but also for anyone with responsibility for young people. It is in some ways harder to deal with than coping with a life-threatening physical illness. Concerns about self-harm or suicide are often hidden, even from those closest to us, for many reasons including the stigma which surrounds self-harm and suicide, and sometimes from a primitive belief that putting words on something may in some magical way make it happen. Adults in such situations often feel powerless to do anything to help the young person. If they are parents, they often feel great sadness to see their son or daughter struggling in this way, but also often feel guilty and alone, angry and worried about how the young person's behaviour is affecting other children in the family. Teachers and childcare staff wonder how they can help young people who self-harm, and also worry about its effects on other young people in their care.

This book is written for parents, guardians, foster parents, care staff, teachers, youth workers – anyone who is concerned about a young person at risk of self-harm or suicidal behaviour. The aim of the book is to support them and to help them realize that their support is hugely important to the young people in their care. The book is based on many years' experience of working with young people who have self-harmed or attempted suicide, and with their families and carers, from whom many of the ideas in the book have come.

WHAT IS DELIBERATE SELF-HARM?

There are a number of terms used which can cause confusion. Terms such as 'attempted suicide', 'parasuicide', or 'DSH' are used, and people wonder what the differences are between them. Deliberate self-harm (DSH) refers to any deliberate act which people engage in with the intention of causing harm to themselves. Such acts include cutting themselves, taking overdoses of tablets or other substances, banging their heads on walls, attempting to hang or strangle themselves, and a range of other behaviours. Sometimes these acts are truly driven by an attempt to die by suicide, but more often they are not – they may have a variety of other motivating forces behind them. The term 'parasuicide' is rarely used now, and there is no generally accepted definition of it. It has been replaced by and large by the term 'DSH'. 'Attempted suicide' is the term used when the person's DSH was obviously suicidal in intent, but which did not result in death by suicide.

Some of the confusion around terminology arises because it is often not possible to be really clear about the motivation for the person's DSH. In some cases it is clearly driven by suicidal intent – such as when people take steps to plan what they are going to do (e.g. buying a rope or tablets), planning to carry out the act when they are sure they won't be disturbed or found, or leaving a suicide note. In other cases the person who engages in DSH is clearly not suicidal, such as self-cutting that is done primarily to become a member of a group where this is accepted behaviour, as sometimes happens among adolescents. Between these two extremes lie the majority of young people with DSH, who are often unclear themselves about how suicidal they were when they engaged in DSH. Occasionally young people who are not truly suicidal do die or seriously damage themselves because they misunderstand the risks associated with the behaviour they engage in. Examples include young people who take an overdose of paracetamol, without being aware of the risks of liver damage associated with this.

SUICIDAL OR NOT SUICIDAL?

Jenni is 15 and has just broken up with her boyfriend of six months. To put it her way, she has been 'dumped'. This was her first boyfriend, and their relationship was intense, with some wonderful times, and lots of rows and 'mini-breakups'. However, this seems final. Her boyfriend told her he did not want to continue the relationship, that he felt too tied down, and this conversation happened in the cold light of day, not after a row.

Jenni is distraught. She cannot imagine life without him. She is in intense emotional pain. Her friends try in vain to console her, but nothing helps to ease the pain. She buys a small bottle of vodka, goes home, drinks the vodka and takes an overdose of tablets from the bathroom cupboard. She does not know what they are, but just wants the pain to end.

Jenni's mother hears her vomiting in the bathroom, and when she goes up, Jenni tells her what she has done. She is brought to the accident and emergency department, where the tablets she took are identified, and she receives medical treatment. At that time, when she is under the influence of alcohol, she tells staff she wishes she had died. However, the next day when she is sober, she says she is glad she did not die, and is sorry for the upset she has caused her mother. Her mother is confused and does not know what to think.

HOW COMMON IS DELIBERATE SELF-HARM?

The statistics we have about DSH come from two sources – studies of those who attend hospital accident and emergency departments for treatment following DSH, and studies that ask young people in the community if they have engaged in DSH.

Hospital studies show that DSH in young people is on the increase in most Western cultures, and that children as young as eight or nine are presenting with DSH. In hospital studies, the most common type of DSH is by overdose, followed by cutting. In very young children under 12, boys and girls are almost equally represented, while in the teenage years DSH is somewhat more common in girls, but boys seem to be catching up. Community studies are generally done by questionnaires, and are often done with school or college students. One such study of over 6000 UK school-going adolescents, carried out by Professor Keith Hawton and colleagues at the Oxford Centre for Suicide Research, showed that just over 13 per cent of them had engaged in DSH (Hawton *et al.* 2002). A similar study, the Lifestyle and Coping Survey, which involved almost 4000 Irish adolescents, showed that 9 per cent had engaged in self-harm and of these less than one in ten had sought medical attention (Sullivan *et al.* 2004).

Those who attend hospital with DSH probably represent the more serious cases in terms of needing medical treatment, but it is hard to know whether they are more serious in terms of suicidal risk, because very little is known about those who self-harm but do not come to medical attention.

The studies described show that DSH is quite common, but throw little light on why it seems to be so much more common in recent years. There are no accurate figures of rates of DSH 20 years ago, but most professionals with many years' experience of working with young people in mental health services recall that DSH was an infrequent problem then, whereas now it is an everyday occurrence in most services.

WHO IS AT RISK OF DSH?

Risk factors include age (DSH can occur before puberty, but becomes much more common in the teenage years); gender (DSH is more common in girls, but also occurs in boys where the rate is increasing); where the young person has a history of mental health or behavioural difficulties, or has been abused physically or sexually; those who are experiencing academic or social problems at school; those who are misusing alcohol or drugs; where there is a family history of DSH in close relatives; and where the young person has engaged in DSH in the past.

These are some of the more important risk factors, but it is important to remember that young people with a combination of risk factors are in general more at risk than those with a single risk factor. We know little about what combinations or what sequences of risk factors convey greatest risk, but because we know there are risks associated with repeated DSH, it is worth intervening early to try to prevent that pattern of behaviour from developing.

We know much less about factors that protect young people from engaging in DSH, but there are some studies showing that there is an association between family support and warmth, and good parent–child communication and a reduced risk of DSH (e.g. Cooper *et al.* 2005; Harrington *et al.* 2006).

WHY DO YOUNG PEOPLE HARM THEMSELVES?

There are a few studies which have asked young people who have harmed themselves why they did it (e.g. Sullivan 2004). The reasons given are many and varied, but almost all said that it was a way of coping with very painful feelings and that it made them feel better for a short time. This may seem hard to understand, but young people explain that the physical pain of harming themselves in some way relieves their mental pain. The relief does not last long, however. The mental pain returns and can lead to further self-harm. Other reasons given include a need to punish themselves, or a need to 'feel something' if their feelings are numbed. Some young people say they needed to show someone else how badly they were feeling, although this is unusual, as self-harm is generally a secret activity that is kept hidden from others. Most say they were not suicidal when they self-harmed, but a small number say they wanted to end their lives. Some say they genuinely don't know why they did it, and it may be that these young people are just not able to put their feelings into words.

DOES SELF-HARM LEAD TO SUICIDE?

DSH does not lead to suicide in the vast majority of cases, but the risk of suicide is higher in those who have engaged in DSH than in those who have not. This is particularly so for young people who engage in repeated DSH. Somewhere between 40 and 60 per cent of young people who die by suicide have a history of DSH. Suicide is the major concern of most parents and carers of young people who have self-harmed. While it is not always possible to prevent suicide in someone who is determined to end their life in this way, this book contains a lot of information about how to improve communication with young people, help them to access services, and 'walk the road' with them towards a healthier way of coping with life's challenges.

WILL THE YOUNG PERSON CONTINUE TO SELF-HARM?

A recent community study involving almost 2000 adolescents in Australia showed that 8 per cent had engaged in self-harm in adolescence, but when they were followed up into early adulthood, over 90 per cent had stopped (Moran *et al.* 2011). This is encouraging information for young people who self-harm and for those who care for them, but more research is needed about what helps young people to stop self-harming.

HOW DO MENTAL HEALTH PROFESSIONALS ASSESS SOMEONE WHO HAS DELIBERATELY SELF-HARMED?

When a young person attends an accident and emergency department with DSH, the first priority is to attend to any physical health needs and to provide any medical treatment necessary. This may involve cleaning and dressing wounds, and suturing if necessary; or if an overdose has been taken, giving medication to prevent drugs from being absorbed into the blood stream, measuring blood levels of whatever has been taken, giving antidotes if such exist, and monitoring heart function, breathing and blood pressure. Mental health assessment can only be carried out when the young person is fully conscious and medically stable. Mental health assessment generally involves interviews with the young person and with the parent or carer. The purpose of the interviews is to enable the professional to assess the young person's suicidal risk, to advise if admission to hospital is needed to allow for further assessment or intervention, and to advise what follow-up care is needed. The strengths and difficulties of the young person and the family will be asked about in the assessment, and this may be a difficult and seemingly very intrusive interview for parents, particularly where the DSH has seemed to come 'out of the blue'. The professional is trying to assess if there is a risk of suicide if the young person is discharged home, the ability of those caring for the young person to provide support, and whether or not there is an underlying mental health disorder which may need treatment in its own right.

In most cases the young person will be discharged following this assessment, with arrangements being put in place for follow-up support. This may be with the family doctor, or the young person may be referred for counselling or to the local child and adolescent mental health service (CAMHS).

WHAT ABOUT CONFIDENTIALITY?

The mental health professional carrying out the assessment will have explained to the parents or carers and to the young person that the information given by the young person will be kept confidential, except in situations where the professional considers there is a serious risk to the young person. Suicidal thoughts or acts, or serious self-harm would be considered situations in which confidentiality could be breached in the best interest of the young person. In order to protect young people, parents or guardians need to know if they are at risk in this way.

The National Institute for Clinical Excellence (NICE) in the United Kingdom has published guidelines for professionals on best practice in the management of self-harm at all ages, including in children and young people, and also guidance for young people and their parents, carers or advocates on what to expect when attending services for treatment of self-harm (NICE 2004).

The Appendix contains details of some useful websites that provide information about self-harm for young people and the adults in their lives.

CHAPTER 2

RECOGNIZING AND RESPONDING TO SELF-HARM AND SUICIDAL BEHAVIOUR IN YOUNG PEOPLE

For adults with responsibility for young people, suicide attempts and self-harm are amongst the most frightening problems to be faced. This chapter outlines the signs that may indicate that a young person is at risk of self-harm, as well as describing in concrete terms what can be done in situations where self-harm or suicidal behaviour are immediate concerns. It outlines how to get professional help and how to encourage and support a young person to ask for such help.

CONNIE'S STORY

Connie is 14, and has recently moved to a new school, where she is in the second year. Her parents have informed the school that she was unhappy in her previous school because of bullying and exclusion by the other girls, but that they got help for her, and she is 'fine' now. Her Year Head is not so sure that she is 'fine'. She is struggling with her school work, and appears not to be making any friends in her class. She is regularly absent, and comes in with notes from home saying she has been unwell, but without further explanation. She looks pale and tired most of the time, and is excused from after-school sport at her parents' request. She rarely speaks in class, but her essays seem pre-occupied with sadness and death.

One Monday morning another student reports that Connie is upset and is vomiting in the toilet.

Continued on p.25.

KERRIE'S STORY

Kerrie aged 15 lives in a residential care home, and has been 'in care' since the age of 10. Since coming into care, she has lived with four different foster families, but each placement has broken down because of her difficult behaviour. She cannot accept rules, has stolen from her foster families and from shops, goes binge drinking regularly, and sometimes does not return home at night. She becomes verbally and sometimes physically aggressive if staff try to prevent her doing what she wants to do.

Kerrie cuts herself on a regular basis, usually following a row with a peer or staff member. The cuts are usually superficial, but the cutting episodes are becoming more frequent, and staff are concerned about what this may lead to, and also about the effect on the other young people in the residential care home, all of whom are young people 'at risk'.

ED'S STORY

Ed is 13 and has recently moved from primary school to a new secondary school. He was very popular with teachers in primary school, as he is highly intelligent, with a great interest in history and maths, at which he used to spend hours on the internet researching his various projects. He did not have any friends in primary school, but was regarded with some awe by his classmates, and he seemed to be content and fulfilled.

Things have changed since moving to secondary school. He seems very unhappy, and his interest in history and maths has waned a lot. He now spends hours lying on his bed, apparently doing nothing, and has become very isolated, despite his parent's attempts to get him to join in family activities. He says he hates school, but will not say why. He has told his brother that he wishes he was dead.

His teachers have expressed concern, as he rarely contributes in class, and spends break times alone. There is a chess club in his school, set up to provide a venue for like-minded students to meet, but Ed refuses to attend. Ed's parents and teachers wonder how to help him.

All of the young people described above are 'at risk' of DSH. Connie sounds as if she is struggling with depression and may have taken an overdose, Kerrie has behaviour problems involving a variety of risk-taking behaviours, while Ed's change in mood and behaviour warrants further assessment, and may be related to his increasing awareness of his difference from his peers, to bullying, to the onset of an adolescent mental health disorder, or to a combination of these and other factors.

RECOGNIZING WARNING SIGNS

There are rarely no 'warning signs' that a young person is suicidal, although we all know of situations in which a young person has died by suicide which was said to have come 'out of the blue'. This does happen occasionally, but research has shown that most young people who die by suicide have had pre-existing mental health difficulties that have often been unrecognized and untreated. 'Psychological autopsy studies' involve detailed interviews with those closest to the person who died by suicide, in an attempt to piece together the months leading up to the person's death. Such studies are not easy to do, as they involve intruding on families, friends, colleagues, workmates and peers at a time when they are grieving and suffering themselves. Studies of this type have been done in the USA by Professor David Shaffer (Shaffer *et al.* 1996), and in the United Kingdom by Professor Keith Hawton (Hawton, Houston and Shepperd 1999), renowned experts in suicidal behaviour in young people. These studies have shown that death by suicide is much more common in young men than in young women, and that about 70 per cent of young people who die by suicide have a mental health disorder, most often depression, and that alcohol and/or drug misuse have often been present, along with legal problems and long-term difficulties with education and relationships. These findings are generalizations and do not by any means apply to all young people who die by suicide, but they do make us realize the importance of early recognition and support for young people, particularly young men, with difficulties in a number of areas of their lives.

Recognizing that a young person is struggling and may be suicidal can be very helpful, and may prevent a suicide attempt or other type of self-harm. Increasing isolation, marked mood changes, increasing anger, increasing use of alcohol or drugs, decline in performance at school, college or work, deterioration in self-care – these are all pointers to someone who may be at risk of DSH. All of these behaviours tend to push people away from the person at risk, and it can be very difficult to intervene with someone who appears to be at best disinterested and at worst actively resisting getting help. However, just noticing that the person is struggling, and reaching out to him may in itself have a 'holding' effect on someone in despair. A quiet word, such as 'Things seem to be a bit rough for you at the moment – anything I can do to help?' is almost guaranteed to elicit the response 'I'm fine', but the message of concern and support conveyed can help to sustain a young person. This reaching out can be done by parents, family members, friends, teachers or others in contact with young people at risk. This may seem so obvious that it is not worth mentioning, but people are often so afraid of 'opening up a can of worms' that they shy away from any type of personal communication with a troubled young person.

PRACTICAL PRECAUTIONS

Many overdoses and other acts of self-harm are done on impulse, by a vulnerable young person following a row or other upset. It makes a lot of sense to 'spring clean' the house and dispose of any medication that is not essential, and to ensure that essential medication is kept in a locked cupboard. Firearms should not be kept in the house at all, but if they must be, it is vital that they are kept in a secure situation to which the young person does not have access.

Those who are determined to harm themselves will find a way to do it, despite the most rigorous precautions, but simple, commonsense precautions may prevent the much more common scenario where a young person acts on impulse.

RESPONDING TO WARNING SIGNS

How best to respond to warning signs depends on their seriousness, the context in which they are happening, and the relationship with the young person. There are a few particular warning signs that suicide may be imminent, but these are rare. They include being preoccupied with the suicide of a friend or admired figure, or giving away possessions, telling people that they are considering or planning suicide, or making elaborate preparations. In a crisis situation such as this, it is important to make your concerns known to the person at risk, to try to remain calm, not to be afraid to ask the person if he is considering suicide, and to stay with him until he is feeling safer and a plan is in place for him to get the help he needs.

DEALING WITH CRISIS SITUATIONS

Ms Bryan, Connie's teacher, went to the toilets, having informed the Year Head of the situation. Connie was crying and had obviously been vomiting. Several girls were there, trying to help her. Ms Bryan asked the girls to return to class while she comforted Connie and asked her what had happened. Connie did not answer, but in response to Ms Bryan asking her calmly if she had taken anything, Connie said she had taken tablets at home that morning. Ms Bryan told Connie she would have to go to hospital, and asked the Year Head to inform Connie's mother or father, whoever she could contact, and to call an ambulance. Ms Bryan remained with Connie, quietly reassuring her and helping her to clean herself up. Connie was very frightened and did not want to go in the ambulance when it arrived, saying she would be 'fine'. Ms Bryan accompanied her in the ambulance to the local accident and emergency department. Connie's mother was already there when they arrived, and she took over from Ms Bryan.

Such situations of acute urgency are thankfully rare. It is important to try to remain calm. You are likely to be feeling shocked, even angry, or maybe just numb, but the young person who has harmed himself needs calm adult support at this time. The priority is to attend to the young person's medical needs in a supportive way. For teachers, youth workers and social care workers, it will be necessary to seek the support and advice of a senior colleague with experience of their agency's policy on responding to an acute crisis of this type. Knowing the policy of the agency in advance makes situations such as this somewhat easier to manage. It will be necessary to inform the young person's parent or guardian of the situation, and to ensure in the first instance that appropriate medical care is provided to the young person who has harmed himself. In an acute crisis the most direct route to mental healthcare is often through the local accident and emergency department.

Being the adult in charge in crisis situations like this is a very frightening experience. Having to be calm and 'cope' can take its toll. Being able to talk it over with someone after the event can help the person to 'debrief' and to feel better. This may be a partner or friend, or it may be a mental health professional – someone whom you trust and who is there for you, to whom you can express how you really feel. It is normal to feel very angry with a young person who has put you through something like this, even if it is your son or daughter. Being able to express your fears, frustrations, guilt or anger can be very helpful.

DEALING WITH CONCERNS ABOUT SUICIDAL BEHAVIOUR

A much more common situation is one where there is a troubled young person whose behaviour is a cause for concern to the adults in his life, where there may or may not be some risk of suicidal behaviour. What is the best way to help if that is the case?

Talking to others who know the young person

It can help to get concerns into perspective by discussing them with someone else who knows the young person. This may be a family member, a teacher, a sports coach, a youth worker – anyone who sees the young person in a different context from yours. This is not being disloyal to the young person, and can be framed in general language, such as 'Lisa seems a bit low at home [or at school, gym, etc., depending on context] at the moment – I am wondering how you find her?' It may be that the young person presents a totally different picture in a different context. For example, a young person may be withdrawn, hostile and easily irritated at home, but be involved, helpful and functioning well in school. This may help to reassure a worried parent. It does not mean there are no problems, but it makes it less likely that there is a serious mental health problem.

Talking to the young person

This can be difficult, and there is no 'right' or 'wrong' way to do it. Teenagers are struggling to become independent of parents, and the last thing they want is someone trying to get 'into their heads'. A low-key approach seems to work best, where you express your concerns in concrete terms, such as 'I am a bit worried about you because I have noticed you are spending an awful lot of time in your room, and I'm wondering if things are OK?' Be prepared for the usual 'I'm fine' answer, delivered with varying degrees of irritation! Many of the young people I have worked with have said how much they appreciate their parents showing their concern in this way, although almost all of them appeared to rebuff the concerns at the time.

KEVIN'S STORY

'Sometimes I would feel depressed, and when I'd get home I'd just go up and sit in my room for ages, and maybe cry sometimes, like just by myself... My dad might come up and ask me what was wrong but I'd just ignore him. I'd wanted to talk to him, but I wanted him to know what was wrong without me having to say it out. I told him eventually that I was having hassle at school and he helped me to think about solutions.'

Informal help

Adult support can be very helpful to a young person who is troubled, and is often underestimated. Support provided by parents can be invaluable, but as already explained, this may be unacceptable to the young person because of his developmental need to struggle for independence. Sometimes contact with and interest shown by someone who is less emotionally involved is much more acceptable. An adult who 'keeps an eye out' for the young person, who checks in with him regularly, who may have a shared interest, and who does not expect deep conversations about how he is feeling, may provide invaluable support, often without knowing he is doing so. This is particularly so for young men, who find it notoriously difficult to talk about their feelings and frequently refuse to attend counselling or other services. Such adult support might be provided by a relative, a youth worker, a teacher, a coach – any adult who has an interest in the young person.

Young people who cannot accept such support from parents are often able to do so from someone who is not as close to them. Some parents who are aware of this have found it useful to share their concerns (or some of them) with another adult in the young person's life, with a request that they would 'look out' for their son or daughter.

More formal help

More formal help is needed for young people who have already engaged in some form of DSH, or who have talked about suicide or indicated that it is on their minds, or whose life is being significantly affected by their difficulties – for example missing out on education through being unable or unwilling to attend school – or whose health is being affected through misuse of alcohol or drugs. More formal help may also be needed in situations where the young person's behaviour is having a very negative impact on those close to him, for example through aggressive behaviour, threats of self-harm, etc.

The type of professional help will depend on the nature of the difficulties which the young person is experiencing, and the services which are available locally. Most areas in the United Kingdom and Ireland have youth services which provide counselling or psychotherapy, and also have Child and Adolescent Mental Health Services (CAMHS) which provide treatment and family support for young people with more serious mental health difficulties. Being informed about what is available and how to access services is an important first step. This information can be provided by family doctors or social services departments. A family doctor who knows the young person can be an invaluable asset, and may be prepared to see the young person and to advise on whether onward referral is needed.

Approaching getting help with the young person

This can be difficult. Young people who are struggling with their emotions and behaviour often have very mixed feelings about 'getting help'. They often know they need help and very much want it, but are fearful of what it will involve, afraid they will be told they are 'mad' or that they may be 'put away'. If they are depressed they will probably feel that nothing could help anyway.

It is a good idea to give some thought to how best to approach the idea of getting help with the young person, to know what is available and how to go about getting an appointment, and what will be involved. It helps if the important adults in the young person's life are in agreement about the need for help. This will involve discussion between parents of young people living at home, and among staff teams and management for young people in residential care.

The best time to broach the subject of getting help is when you are calm and well informed. You might say something like 'I'm worried about you because I notice that you have missed a lot of school/seem very low in yourself/ have stopped going out/are drinking a lot/seem very angry most of the time. I feel we need help to sort this out, and I've arranged an appointment for us to meet with XXX next week to see if there is any help available.' Mentioning your concerns based on what you have observed, rather than on what you think the young person may be feeling, seems to work better. Be prepared for an angry denial that there are any problems, and try not to take personally hurtful responses such as 'You're the one with the problem – if it wasn't for you I'd be fine.' A helpful response to that type of remark is to agree that they might be right, and that is one of the reasons why you will be jointly seeking help. Try not to get drawn into a lengthy argument, and be prepared to keep any appointment you have made – even if you have to attend without the young person in the first instance. This approach will usually but not always result in the young person attending for counselling or mental health support. Information on counselling and other approaches to treatment are outlined in Chapter 3, 'Treatment of Self-harm and Suicidal Behaviour'. For further ideas, please see 'He won't accept help' and 'Child protection concerns' in Chapter 7, 'Special Problems'.

CHAPTER **3**

TREATMENT OF SELF-HARM AND SUICIDAL BEHAVIOUR

A variety of treatment approaches have been described for self-harm. Some have been shown to be effective, but there is continuing uncertainty about which is most effective. It is important that treatment is provided for any underlying mental health disorder, though not all young people with self-harm have such disorders.

Despite the fact that DSH is a relatively common problem among young people, there are few studies of how best to treat it. This is not all that surprising, as DSH can vary from, at one end of the spectrum, a one-off incident at a time of upset in a young person's life, to repeated episodes used as a coping mechanism by a young person with a significant mental health disorder, or to a definite attempt to die by suicide at the other end of the spectrum. Also, the studies which have been done have involved young people who have come to the attention of mental health professionals. We know from community surveys that most young people who self-harm do not come to the attention of such professionals, and little or nothing is known about what helps them to stop self-harming, though we do know that more than 90 per cent have stopped by late adolescence (Moran *et al.* 2011).

Many young people who are assessed in accident and emergency departments following self-harm tend not to keep follow-up appointments. They have also been shown to have poorer problem-solving skills than other young people, to be more impulsive, and to have more difficulties regulating their emotional responses. This means that they become more easily overwhelmed by the strength of feelings of hurt, anger, guilt or sadness, and do not have coping mechanisms to deal with such feelings. Various treatment approaches have been developed to try to address some of these difficulties.

SPECIFIC TREATMENTS FOR DSH

A Cochrane Review of the various treatments for DSH has been carried out (Hawton, Townsend *et al.* 1999). Cochrane Reviews are systematic reviews of research in human healthcare and health policy, and are highly respected internationally. This review has shown that, while a number of treatment approaches show promise, there is continuing uncertainty about which approach is most effective, and the review was unable to recommend a particular treatment approach. This is perhaps not surprising, given the many different levels of severity of DSH and the many different factors which contribute to it.

The approaches to treatment covered by the Cochrane Review include:

- Emergency cards
- Problem-solving therapies

- Home-based intervention – The Kerfoot Programme
- Dialectic behaviour therapy
- Developmental group therapy.

Emergency cards

Young people who have been assessed in accident and emergency departments following DSH are given cards with telephone contact details to enable them to access services 24 hours a day, and are encouraged to use them in a crisis. This approach attempts to reduce the rate of repetition of DSH through the immediate provision of support by a mental health professional. It cuts down the rate of repetition of DSH, but is only slightly more effective than a variety of other more general treatment approaches.

Problem-solving therapies

This approach works on the principle that young people's emotional and behavioural difficulties arise from everyday life problems, and that if they can manage their problems more effectively, then their difficulties will be reduced, leading to less self-harm. It deals with the 'here and now', and uses cognitive behavioural therapy (CBT) techniques (see Laura's case study, p.36). It helps young people to understand the link between their emotional and behavioural difficulties and their life problems, and teaches them a specific approach to problem-solving which they are encouraged to apply to current problems in their life. It involves close collaboration between the young person and the therapist, with the young person identifying her problems and setting her own goals, and is generally a short-term therapy over five or six sessions. It has been shown to reduce the rate of repetition of DSH, but again is only slightly more effective than some other treatment approaches.

Home-based family intervention – The Kerfoot Programme

This is a family-based intervention carried out in the young person's home over four sessions. It uses a family-based problem-solving approach with much emphasis on family communication skills. Evaluation has shown it to be no more effective than routine care, but it has more appeal for families. Among a subgroup of young people within the study who had no underlying depressive disorder, there was less suicidal ideation at follow-up in those who received this therapy than in those who received routine care. It tends to be used mainly for young people whose living arrangements are stable, and where there are no significant underlying mental health difficulties.

Dialectic behaviour therapy

This is a long-term intensive therapy approach which has been shown to reduce the rate of DSH and hospital admission in young people and adults where DSH has become a recurrent intractable problem that is interfering very significantly in their ability to get on with life. Dialectic behaviour therapy is an approach which brings together CBT principles with a philosophy of acceptance and validation of the young person's experience. It is expensive, time-consuming and demanding, but has been shown to be more effective and more cost-effective than other approaches with this small group of young people who have often had very damaging life experiences and who tend to be heavy users of health and mental health services, often without much apparent benefit.

Developmental group therapy

This approach involves group therapy to address difficulties that have been shown to be common in the lives of young people with DSH, including peer relationship problems, bullying and family problems. When it was initially evaluated it showed great promise (Wood *et al.* 2001), but more recent evaluation has shown that it is no more effective than routine care in reducing the rate of repetition and the severity of DSH (Green *et al.* 2011).

TREATMENT OF UNDERLYING MENTAL HEALTH DISORDERS

Many studies have shown that between 40 and 70 per cent of young people presenting with DSH have an underlying mental health disorder. This is one of the reasons why it is so important that they have a proper mental health assessment and follow-up. Depression is the most common underlying disorder. Other disorders include behaviour disorders, such as oppositional defiant disorder or conduct disorder, misuse of alcohol or drugs, attention deficit hyperactivity disorder (ADHD), and eating disorders, such as anorexia nervosa or bulimia nervosa. When the underlying disorder is properly treated, the need for self-harm is often significantly reduced.

LAURA'S VICIOUS CYCLE

Laura is a 14-year-old girl who took an overdose of paracetamol one evening at home, when there was no one else in the house. She went to bed and seemed to be asleep when her mother checked on her when she came in. During the night her mother heard her vomiting, and went in to her. Laura told her what she had done, and her mother called an ambulance.

Once Laura had received medical treatment for the overdose, she was interviewed by a psychiatrist from the mental health team. She told the psychiatrist that she had been planning to take the overdose for a few weeks, and had bought the tablets in a few different shops, as the first shop she tried refused to sell her more than one packet. She said she wanted to end her life, as there was no point in living. She had hoped to die when she took the tablets, but had become scared when she started to vomit. She still wished she had died, and was not sure whether or not she would try the same thing again in the future.

Laura's mother, Margaret, told the psychiatrist that she had been worried about Laura for the previous several months, but thought she was 'just being a teenager'. She said that Laura had changed from being a quiet, shy but reasonably happy person, to one who missed many days of school because of aches and pains and not feeling well. Her school work seemed of little interest to her, which surprised her mother, as she had been a very conscientious student in primary school. She had given up going to her youth club, and also her salsa class. She did not seem to have any friends, and was spending hours alone in her room.

Margaret had herself suffered from depression on and off in the past, and wondered if this was what was wrong with Laura. Margaret had tried on many occasions to talk to Laura. When she asked her what was the matter, Laura said 'Nothing' and left the room.

Laura had to remain in hospital for a few days while her liver function tests where monitored, as the paracetamol had caused some liver damage. She met the psychologist on the mental health team for a session each day, and was able to discuss with her the upset she felt about her parents' separation two years ago, and how she could hardly bear to talk to her dad, who she felt had 'left Mum in the lurch'. She had had to change school when her parents separated, and she felt excluded and 'different' in the new school. She said she had lost interest in 'almost everything' and could not think of the last time she had enjoyed anything. She reluctantly agreed to attend the local CAMHS for help with her difficulties, when she was discharged.

Laura attended the CAMHS regularly over the next six months. Her mother attended with her, and her father came to some of the sessions. Laura was very off-hand with her father initially, although she was secretly pleased that he attended. She was told she had depression, but did not really agree with this initially. However, she did agree to attend for CBT sessions to help with her problems. Through work with her therapist she learned about how depression can affect your thinking, making everything seem hopeless and pointless, and can make you always think the worst. This made sense to her. She learned that when depression affects your thinking in this way, it influences your behaviour in a way which makes the depression worse, and you get into a 'vicious cycle'. Through CBT she learned ways to help herself feel better through setting and achieving goals she set herself. These were very small goals initially – her first goal was to watch TV with her mum each evening for at least 15 minutes, rather than spending all evening alone in her room. When she succeeded with this, her confidence improved and she was ready to take on harder goals, such as responding in a positive way at school when one of the girls asked for her help with a maths problem.

While Laura was having her sessions, her parents were having sessions with another therapist who supported them in their efforts to help Laura. They learned about how depression can affect young people, how it is treated and the likely outlook for the future. Laura's mother wondered if she needed anti-depressant medication, and was told that this would be kept in mind, but the current practice in treating depression in young people involves therapy in the first instance, except in those cases where the depression is so severe that the young person cannot engage in therapy. If Laura's depression was not responding to CBT, then anti-depressant medication would be discussed with Laura and her parents. The importance of family communication was discussed, such as noticing small steps in a positive direction, trying not to respond with anger and hostility when Laura said hurtful things to her parents, keeping a connection with her, and not trying to 'talk her out of it', as this tends not to work and to lead to more arguments and conflict.

Laura's mood improved gradually over the next few months. Her parents noticed that she seemed more relaxed and was in better form. She no longer complained of aches and pains and seemed more positive about school. She started to take some interest in hockey at school and became friendly with some of the girls on her team. Her mother heard her singing along to her music in her bedroom one day, and realized she had not heard this for almost a year. Her sessions in the CAMHS were reduced to once a month for three months, and after a further six months she was discharged.

DARREN AND ADHD

Darren had been diagnosed with ADHD at the age of eight, having been referred to the local CAMHS because of his impulsive behaviour and poor concentration in school and at home. Following assessment it was recommended that he receive special help in school, and his parents attended a course for parents of children with ADHD, where they learned about the disorder, and how best to help Darren. The use of medication for ADHD was discussed at that time, but for many reasons Darren's parents were reluctant to consider it.

With the support of his parents and teachers, Darren's difficulties improved and he got through primary school without too much difficulty. When he moved to secondary school his parents wanted him to have a fresh start, so they did not inform his secondary school about his ADHD. Things did not go well in his new school. He was constantly in trouble for giddy, distractible behaviour in the first year, and got a reputation for being a 'messer'. By the time he was in the second year, he had fallen badly behind in his school work, was sent out of class most days, and was 'on report' much of the time. At home he was angry, negative and oppositional, and was constantly arguing with his parents and siblings. Following a particularly bitter row at home he took an overdose of medication he found in the bathroom – it was diazepam (Valium) which had been prescribed for his mother. He told his brother shortly after he had done it, and was brought to the accident and emergency department. During his assessment there, he told the psychiatrist that he did not know why he had taken the tablets, that he was just 'fed up with all the hassle' and that nothing was going right at home or at school. He denied any suicidal thoughts or plans.

He was referred back to the CAMHS he had attended in the past, where it was recommended that further thought be given to medication for his ADHD. Following discussion with members of the ADHD Team, Darren and his parents decided to try medication. It was also decided that a member of the ADHD Team would link up with the school to explain about ADHD and how Darren could be best helped in school.

It took about two months to get the dose of medication right, but once this was achieved, things improved a good deal for Darren. He was able to concentrate better in school, and was encouraged by his Year Head to take up athletics, which helped him to feel calmer inside. With this support his confidence grew, and his behaviour and attitude improved at school and at home.

Darren is now 16 and still needs medication for ADHD. He dislikes having to take it, but realizes that it helps, and in the last few months has taken on responsibility himself for taking the medication. There have been no further episodes of self-harm.

OTHER TYPES OF THERAPY

There are many different types of therapy, including psychodynamic, systemic, cognitive, behavioural, humanistic, art- or drama-based therapies, and many more. While most forms of therapy have been shown to be effective, there is little robust evidence that any one type of therapy is superior to another. What seems to be important is the relationship between the young person and a properly trained, skilled, empathic therapist, who work together over a period of time, with a specific focus (Messer and Wampold 2002). Such therapists are in short supply, but for any young person with repeated DSH and underlying mental health problems, it is well worth making a determined effort to find one.

CHAPTER **4**

WHAT CAN PARENTS AND CARERS DO?

The support provided by those who care for and about young people who self-harm plays a huge role in helping them deal with their difficulties. This chapter looks at ways of making and keeping a connection with the young person, positive communication, fostering a healthy lifestyle and survival skills for parents and carers – the importance of 'self-care'. It also looks realistically at what parents and carers can and can't do.

Those who care for and about young people who self-harm often feel powerless to do anything to help. They may have tried talking to the young person about what might be going on for him, and been angrily rebuffed, making them reluctant to try again. Or they may be afraid to mention their concerns for fear of making a bad situation worse. They may be faced with a young person who seems determined to keep everyone at arm's length by insisting that everything is 'fine', or whose only interaction with those who care about him involves rows and arguments which leave everyone involved feeling hurt, angry and upset. It is easy to become 'mentally paralyzed' in situations like this.

However, research has shown that support can serve to protect young people from DSH. A review of research in this area carried out for Scottish Government Social Research found that having a good relationship with parents protects adolescents against the risk of suicidal behaviour (McLean *et al.* 2008). Another study involving 451 families in the USA showed that warm and communicative behaviours conveyed by mothers protected against suicidal behaviour in their adolescents, and that similar behaviours by fathers protected against adolescent emotional distress (Connor and Rueter 2006). So good communication makes a difference. But communication with a young person where there are concerns about DSH can be difficult. Parents and carers who have concerns about possible DSH, such as Liz, mother of Sandy, whose case study was introduced in Chapter 1, wonder how best to bring up the subject without antagonizing the young person. There is no 'right' or 'wrong' way to do this, but it seems to work best if parents have taken some time planning how best to mention their concerns. It also helps if DSH can be viewed as a means of communication, the message being that all is not well for the young person concerned.

LIZ CONNECTING WITH SANDY

Sandy's response did little to reassure Liz, but made her even more wary of bringing up the subject again. However, the cuts continued to appear, and Liz felt she could no longer remain silent. She planned how she would raise the subject with Sandy when both were relaxed. She knew that Sandy might brush her off again, and made up her mind that she would not take this personally, but would see it as Sandy's wish to deal with her problems in her own way.

One evening when both were in quite good form, Liz mentioned to Sandy that she had noticed that the cuts on her arms were still happening, and that she knew that sometimes people cut themselves when they were going through a tough time. She did not ask Sandy if she was cutting herself, but just said that she was there to help if Sandy wanted to talk about anything. Sandy again said she was 'fine', but without so much anger this time.

Liz went out of her way to keep a connection with Sandy, in a low-key way. If she was going to town, she would ask Sandy if she would like to come. She encouraged her to watch her favourite TV soap downstairs with the family, rather than in her room. She commented on positive things she noticed about Sandy's behaviour, such as how she did not retaliate when her sister called her a name, and how she stuck up for a friend who was being bullied.

Sandy seemed to become gradually more relaxed. The cuts on her arms gradually became less noticeable and after a few months no further cuts appeared. She never opened up to Liz about why she was self-harming nor about what might lie behind it. Liz was none the wiser, but felt that her concern and 'reaching out' to Sandy had made some sort of difference, in a way that she found hard to describe.

MAKING AND KEEPING A CONNECTION WITH THE YOUNG PERSON

Few adolescents want to have heart-to-heart conversations with their parents or carers, but much can be achieved by simply keeping a connection with them. This means showing some interest in what interests them, their friends, what they like to do or not do. This sounds easy, but it is difficult to get the balance right. If it is overdone, the young person may feel smothered and may withdraw further. If underdone (for fear of seeming intrusive or nosey, or for fear of an angry response), it is easy to end up with a situation where there is little or no communication with the young person.

Many parents have spoken of their frustration when the only communication with their teenager seems to involve requests for money or lifts. However, these requests can be seen positively and used as opportunities for communication. There is something about driving with your teenager in the passenger seat which seems to make conversation easier. Maybe it is the fact that it does not require face-to-face contact. It presents the opportunity to talk about neutral topics such as where they are going, what they will be doing, etc. This often leads on to deeper issues, but it is important not to push for this, to take the young person's lead. Requests for money can also lead to conversations about what the money is for, provided this is done in the spirit of genuine curiosity, and not as a means of gathering evidence!

POSITIVE COMMUNICATION

Communication experts tell us that the meaning of what we say is conveyed more by how we say something than by the words we use. Even something as simple as the word 'please' can convey many different meanings, depending on how it is said. When it is said loudly and with anger, it conveys a different message to when it is said quietly and in a neutral tone. Part of my training in managing potentially explosive situations in mental health settings involved paying attention to my facial expression, body language and tone of voice, rather than to what to say. Particularly when emotions are highly charged, more meaning is conveyed by how things are said. Giving space, avoiding threatening body language, and a calm tone of voice can do much to defuse such situations.

Another useful concept is 'pressing the pause button'. This is useful in situations where our natural response is to react with anger to a situation where we feel provoked, and there are many such situations when dealing with troubled young people (see p.63).

JIM AND JACK

Jim arrived home from work after a long day to find his son Jack (15) lying on the sofa, watching TV. There were breakfast and lunch dishes on the living room floor. Jack was wearing a tee shirt and boxers, and it was clear from the picture presented that he had not been to school that day. Jim had encountered this situation many times in the past. He usually reacted initially with sarcastic anger, later with roars and shouts, and on occasions had hit his son, which he bitterly regretted later.

This time he decided to do something different. He changed out of his work clothes, made himself a cup of tea, and planned how best to handle the situation. Meanwhile Jack had got himself dressed and was tidying the living room. Jim calmly said to Jack, 'It's good to see you tidying up before your mum comes in. We both worry about you missing so much school because it will have such an effect on your future. Maybe we could talk about it, and see if anything can be done.'

Jack did not say anything in reply, but was very surprised by his father's reaction. The next day he spoke to Jim, telling him how much he hated school, how difficult he found the school work, and how little point he could see in going to school. Together they worked out a plan that he would attend school as much as he could manage for the next four months, when he would be 16 and could legally leave school. Between now and then his parents would look into what was available for early school leavers, as

Jack had told them he wanted to do something connected with electronics, and they needed to explore what training might be available in this area.

FOSTERING A HEALTHY LIFESTYLE

In recent years research has shown the beneficial effects of exercise on mood as well as on general health. Healthy eating patterns and drinking in moderation are also beneficial for general wellbeing. All the good practice guidelines state that sharing this information should be part of the management of a variety of mental health disorders in young people. Having done this as a professional for many years, I never met any young person who took the advice on board! Even something like going for a walk, which does not cost anything and which you can do on your own, seemed incredibly boring and pointless to most of the young people I have dealt with.

But fostering a healthy lifestyle does have a role. As a parent or carer, you are a role model, and you need to keep yourself as healthy as possible to support your young person through what can be a long and difficult process. Trying to maintain a healthy lifestyle yourself will help with this, as well as modelling something which may impact on young people at a later stage in their lives, when they have come through many of their difficulties.

SURVIVAL SKILLS FOR PARENTS AND CARERS – THE IMPORTANCE OF 'SELF-CARE'

Looking after yourself may be the last thing on your mind if you have a child with DSH. Your mind is likely to be consumed with worries about how he is doing: Will he self-harm again? Is he at risk of suicide? Will he have mental health problems all his life? What does the future hold for him? Such concerns are entirely normal, but worries like this over the long term can take their toll, making it vital that you take steps to look after your own health and wellbeing.

Looking after yourself means going out of your way to take time for yourself, doing something just for you. Keeping up with friends, especially ones with whom you can really be yourself, can be very helpful. Taking up an interest, learning a new skill, doing voluntary work, attending to your spiritual needs, spending time with nature, having a relaxing bath – the list of possibilities is endless. The important thing is to take time to decide what you are going to do, and build it in to your weekly schedule. By doing so, you are not just helping yourself to cope with stress, you are indirectly helping your young person by being in the best possible position to provide the support he needs.

If your stress level is so high that it is seriously interfering with your ability to cope, leading to depression, drinking too much, or being angry all the time, it is well worth seeking help for yourself, separately from any help your young person may be receiving. Your family doctor will be able to advise on this.

REALIZING WHAT YOU CAN AND CAN'T DO

Most parents and carers want to do all they can to help their young person with DSH through their difficulties. Above all you want your child to stop self-harming. Your support is invaluable in this, but you cannot make him stop, nor can you make him confident and happy. As a parent or carer, you can take steps to help sort out issues of bullying, support for academic difficulties, addressing family problems, and getting help for mental health problems. But you cannot make friends for your young person, nor can you make his friends be nicer to him. You cannot make him achieve better in school, or be more comfortable in social situations. You can help to keep hope alive, with the knowledge that most young people with DSH come through their difficulties, and have stopped self-harming by late adolescence or early adulthood.

CHAPTER **5**

SELF-HARM AND THE FAMILY

The family as a whole is deeply affected by a child's self-harm, but can be a source of support and healing. This chapter focuses on the whole family's needs and how everyone can pull together to help. It looks at sharing information with family members, supporting siblings, keeping family life going, dealing with family problems and 'self-care'.

The family is a unique system where the behaviour and emotional responses of one member affect, and are affected by, everyone else's behaviour and emotional responses. Parents who are coping with the distress of a young person who is self-harming have, in addition, the worry about the effects on other family members. Frequent situations which arise include: how much to tell other children about what is happening to the young person who self-harms; how to cope with the anger often expressed by siblings about the 'special treatment' which the young person who self-harms is getting; how to support siblings who are often anxious; how to manage when parents have very different viewpoints about how to handle family situations; and how to cope with conflicting advice from family members.

In an ideal world parents would support each other, encouraging each other and being sensitive to one another's needs, so that when one parent becomes overwhelmed, the other would be there to take over. In this ideal family, siblings would show understanding and empathy towards their sibling who self-harms, and reach out to help in any way they could. Grandparents would be available without being intrusive, and offer practical as well as emotional support. However, the real world is far from ideal, and the scenario below is much more realistic!

KATE'S STORY

Kate is a 14-year-old girl who has been cutting her forearms on and off over the past year. She lives with her mother, her older brother Des, who is 16, and her half-sister Bonny, who is four. Kate's father lives nearby, and Kate and Des have had open access to him over many years. His partner has recently had a new baby, which Kate seemed to be happy about, but it has meant that he is not as available to Kate or Des as he used to be.

Kate's mother, Clare, is at the end of her tether trying to cope with all the demands on her. She has had to take a lot of time off work to bring Kate to counselling, and she wonders if the counselling is doing any good. Bonny has become clingy, whiney and demanding, and has started to refuse to go to bed at night, having previously had no problems in this area. Kate's relationship with Des, who knows about the self-harm, is strained, as he is angry all the time and calls Kate 'a spoiled cow'. Clare feels she is getting little support from Kate's dad, who has implied that he thinks Kate is 'just looking for attention'. This has further angered Clare, who secretly agrees that part of Kate's problems involves needing more attention from her dad. Kate's maternal grandmother does not know about the self-harm, but is critical of Clare for being 'too soft' on the children.

Continued on p.55.

SHARING INFORMATION WITH FAMILY MEMBERS

Even if siblings have not been told about their sister's or brother's DSH, they will sense an atmosphere in the home. In general it is best to be open with siblings, but this is not always possible. With very young children, a simple explanation such as 'Kate is a bit sad at the moment, and we are trying to help her' may be enough. How much to tell older siblings will depend on the views of the young person with DSH, who may wish to keep private information about her self-harm. If this is the case, it is important to respect her wishes, but it will be necessary to discuss with her what information can be conveyed to siblings. If siblings know that their brother or sister is 'going through a tough time' they are much more likely to be supportive.

For parents who are not living together, the situation can be complicated. If parents have joint guardianship, they both have the legal right to know. Even where there is no joint guardianship, you may, as the parent who is the legal guardian, feel that the young person's other parent needs to know, particularly where the young person is spending time with that parent. This presents problems in situations where the young person does not want 'anyone' to know. In general the wishes of the young person should be respected as far as possible, except in situations where you as a parent feel that the risk to your son or daughter is such that another adult who has responsibility for your child needs to know. You need to act in what you consider to be the best interests of your child. If you need to go against the wishes of your child, you should explain your decision to her, and not go behind her back.

You need all the support you can get from your extended family, but they may not need to know all the details about your young person's difficulties. Relatives and friends who are parents themselves will understand that most parents go through times when family life is difficult, when the support of an offer to babysit, a listening ear, or just the opportunity to 'get away from it all' for a few hours can make all the difference.

SUPPORTING SIBLINGS

Supporting older siblings involves giving them time, allowing them to talk about their anger and distress, without putting pressure on them to talk if they don't want to. It involves 'active listening' which means listening honestly, without trying to talk them out of their anger or upset, but indicating that you can understand why they may be feeling that way. It means answering their questions if you can, but being honest when you don't have answers. With younger siblings, much patience is required to cope with clingy, demanding behaviour. A simple explanation such as described above may help them to make sense of the tense atmosphere at home.

Seeking help from the other parent, who may be able to give more time to all the children, can make things easier.

KEEPING FAMILY LIFE GOING

It is helpful if family routines of mealtimes, homework, after-school activities, etc. can be kept going. This is harder than it sounds, as life with a young person who is self-harming can seem to lurch from one crisis to the next. Birthday celebrations, family outings and holidays are often put on hold if the young person with DSH is unwilling or unable to participate. But perhaps a relative or friend could step in to be with a young person who cannot be left on her own, so that these important family events can still happen.

This is where any extra support you can get, from friends, family or professionally, may make a big difference for all the family.

DEALING WITH FAMILY PROBLEMS

Chronic marital discord, excessive drinking or drug misuse by a family member, domestic violence – these and other family problems often seem insoluble, but they may be having a big impact on the children. Sometimes in families with these problems, they are not talked about at all, usually out of fear, and maybe because they do seem so insoluble. As a parent, you may have 'learned to live' with the problem, but it may be very different for your son or daughter. Acknowledging that such problems exist is a major step in dealing with them. The lead for this will have to come from you as a parent, and this may be the first step in trying to tackle such problems.

LOOKING AFTER YOURSELF – 'SELF-CARE'

Children need cared-for parents as much as they need parents to care for them. The best way to help your children grow up to be confident people with high self-esteem is for you as their parent to model this – that is, to take steps to value and look after yourself.

Self-care and personal renewal are basically about achieving balance in your life. They are about trying to ensure that you address your different needs in a balanced way. There are four dimensions of self-care and personal renewal that we need to address on an ongoing basis in order to manage stress and have a balanced life: physical, mental, emotional and spiritual. Physical activities might include taking exercise, walking, jogging, or playing a sport. Mental activities involve keeping your mind stimulated with other interests, such as reading, watching films or learning new things. Emotional activities include keeping in contact with friends, doing something to foster intimate relationships, such as having a special night out with your partner, or doing self-nurturing things – maybe having a long relaxing bath or a new hair-do. Spiritual activities might involve spending time alone or in nature, taking time for personal reflection or meditation. The important thing is to try to address all these areas, and build them into your regular routine. This may seem completely impossible, even selfish, particularly for parents coping with crisis situations, but looking after yourself really does make a difference. Why not set aside sometime this week to think about what you could do in your own life to look after yourself?

CLARE AND KATE

Clare felt things could not go on the way they were. She had started drinking cans of lager at night to help her sleep, but this wasn't really helping, and was causing more rows between herself and Des, who had accused her of being 'an alco'. Even though she was very fearful of what it might involve, she decided to go for counselling for herself. She had no idea where to go, but her GP recommended a counsellor, and she plucked up the courage to make an appointment.

It took Clare a while to get used to the counselling. She had been hoping the counsellor would tell her how to get things back on track, but it wasn't like that. Instead, the counsellor encouraged her and gave her the confidence to work out herself what she could do to change the things which were causing her most upset. A few weeks after she started the counselling, Clare decided she needed to be more open with Kate and explain to her how upsetting she found her self-cutting. She did this calmly, not in the context of a row, and not with demands that Kate stop – she had tried that before and it had not worked. She also spoke with Des, explaining that she could understand his anger with Kate, and saying that she also often felt very angry with her. She told Des that his constant belittling and name-calling of Kate was adding to everyone's stress, and she asked him if he could think of something positive he could do that might help. She enlisted his help, and Kate's, in getting the dinner each evening, giving her time to read a story to Bonny, which helped Bonny settle to bed more easily. The hardest thing of all was talking honestly to Kate and Des's father, as she did not want him to know how hard she had been finding things. With the support of her counsellor, she decided to be more open with him, and to seek his support in helping more with the children. A friend asked her if she would join her in taking up kick boxing, and they went together to weekly classes, which Clare found provided a complete break from the problems at home, and also helped her to 'let off steam'!

There were no miracle transformations or overnight quick fixes, and there were lots of setbacks, but things did gradually improve. Looking back a year later, Clare was surprised when she realized that she was feeling a lot stronger. It had been over three months since Kate had last cut herself, and Kate, Des and Bonny seemed happier. Clare still had fears about how Kate would cope with the future, but the fears were no longer dominating her life. She is still doing the kick boxing!

CHAPTER **6**

DEALING WITH DISCIPLINE ISSUES

Everyday discipline issues can present huge problems where there are concerns about self-harm or suicidal behaviour. This chapter will help parents and carers decide what discipline issues need to be addressed, and what can be 'let go'. It will help parents and carers to speak up assertively when this needs to be done, and will guide them in helping young people learn from rules and consequences.

MEGAN'S STORY

Megan took an overdose when she was 14, following a row with her mother over not being allowed to go to a disco. Her mother felt she was too young at the time, and had been having problems with Megan who had been coming in late and refusing to say where she had been. The overdose led to Megan being hospitalized overnight, and Megan and her mother had attended a teen counselling service for a few sessions after this. Both found the sessions there helpful.

For a few months after the overdose, Megan knew she would not be allowed go to the disco, and did not ask, but it is now coming up to Halloween and Megan wants to go to the same disco, insisting that all her friends are going. Her mother still has concerns about the disco – she has heard horror stories about what goes on at it, despite the fact that it is a young teens' disco, and is supposed to be alcohol- and drug-free. She does not want Megan to go, but is terrified of the consequences of saying 'no'. She definitely does not want a repeat of what happened the last time.

Continued on p.65.

Everyone knows that teenagers need boundaries, and that part of being a teenager involves pushing against those boundaries. But everyday discipline issues like the one above take on a whole new dimension when dealing with a young person with self-harm or suicidal behaviour. What is a parent or carer to do when saying 'no' runs the risk of further self-harm or suicidal behaviour? Of course, you need to say 'no' when the young person's health, wellbeing or safety are at issue, but some of the points below may be helpful in considering when and how best to do this.

'NORMAL' ADOLESCENCE

Adolescence is the time in life when a young person struggles to establish his own identity, separate from that of those he has been closest to in childhood. This often leads him to have very different views to those of his parents or carers, and to seek acceptance by a peer group whose views and lifestyle he may value above all others, and to whom he is exceptionally loyal. This is the time when 'looking good', which often means looking as much like valued peers as possible, is vitally important. It is the time when adult attitudes and standards are questioned and rebelled against. Teenagers are idealistic, and are notoriously good at picking up on the hypocrisy of the adult world, whereby at times we all say one thing and do the opposite, or are most exercised about behaviour in our children which we also engage in ourselves. Sexual development leads to bodily and emotional changes, which, combined with the need for peer group acceptance, may lead to sexual behaviour that is shocking for parents or carers, and that may place the young person at risk of unwanted pregnancy or sexually transmitted disease. Adolescent mood swings can lead to emotional highs and lows which are baffling to adults.

Thinking back to one's own adolescence can sometimes help when confronted by adolescent behaviour that is particularly frightening, anger-inducing, hurtful or just plain bewildering. Remember the profound preoccupation with yourself and your appearance, the terrible anxiety of waiting for the phone to ring, the desolation when it didn't, the loneliness at times? And at other times, the feeling that you could do anything, that life was wonderful? We probably never again experience the same intensity of feeling in adult life, and maybe we would not want to, but remembering how we felt as adolescents can help us to understand and begin to make sense of some adolescent behaviour such as DSH.

PARENTING STYLE

There is good evidence that an 'authoritative' parenting style is associated with the best outcomes for children and young people. Authoritative parents have a close relationship with their children, and have high expectations of their children's behaviour. They are warm and nurturing, they encourage independence, they listen to their children and encourage them to express their opinions, even when they don't agree with them. They monitor and supervise their child, and even in adolescence they have a good idea who their child's friends are, and where he is and what he is up to. They have clear rules, and have consequences which are enforced when these rules are broken. The rules are explained and discussed with adolescents, who are listened to and have input into decision-making, but authoritative parents are in charge.

It is not surprising that children brought up by authoritative parents have better outcomes than those reared in families where parents are very permissive, or the other extreme – very controlling and authoritarian. For parents to be authoritative, they need to be warm and nurturing, and to have good emotional control themselves. Often without being aware of it, they then model this behaviour for their children, who take it in or 'internalize' it, such that it becomes their own style of behaviour.

From the descriptions above, it sounds as if authoritative parents are perfect human beings, maybe even saints! The research on parenting styles uses questionnaires completed by parents and children which ask how parents generally respond to or handle particular situations. Or sometimes the researchers ask parents and children to complete a joint task, and they observe and rate how parents behave during such tasks. The researchers do not live with the families and observe what goes on 24 hours a day. If they did, they would probably see that no parent is 'authoritative' all the time. Every parent has moments of undue permissiveness ('Oh, go on then – anything for a quiet life'), or the opposite extreme ('You will do it because I say so'). It is the overall, general style of parenting that matters, and authoritative parents seem to have happier, more balanced and better-behaved children.

Foster carers and childcare workers, who are at the front line in caring for children in the care of the local authority, are usually trained to use an 'authoritative' style with the children in their care. Their task is far from straightforward, as many of these children will have had very damaging experiences of abuse or neglect that have impaired their ability to trust adults, to respond to warmth and nurturing, and to control their emotional responses. Even with such children, the calm, consistent, fair, predictable and encouraging nature of the authoritative approach seems to work best, though immense patience is required.

LISTENING TO YOUNG PEOPLE

Very few young people with DSH are good at talking to those closest to them about what lies behind their self-harm. If they had the words, and could talk in this way, they might not need to engage in self-harm. 'Active' listening is a type of listening which seems to work best in encouraging young people to talk. It involves being available when the young person wants to talk, and *really listening*, not trying to watch TV or read the paper at the same time! It means being interested in what the young person has to say, not butting in or giving your point of view, and not offering solutions unless asked.

ACTIVE LISTENING

Chloe arrives home from school in a bad mood. She storms into the kitchen, throws her bag on the floor, and growls, 'That Miss Jones, she is such a bitch! She gave me detention today for absolutely nothing. She has it in for me, she hates me.'

Pat, Chloe's mother, feels some sympathy for Miss Jones, as she knows how challenging Chloe can be. She is also annoyed at Chloe for throwing her bag on the floor, and she knows that when Chloe arrives home from school in this state, the whole family is in for a difficult evening. She anticipates yet another phone call from the school tomorrow, which fills her with dread. She feels like saying angrily, 'Don't throw your bag on the floor. How many times have I asked you not to do that?', and following it up with, 'You must have been doing something. Teachers don't give detention for nothing.' Instead, she takes a deep breath herself, and says calmly, 'It sounds as if you have had a tough day. How about a cup of tea?' as she put the kettle on.

Chloe sits down, and they both have a cup of tea. Chloe speaks at length about how much she hates Miss Jones, her maths teacher. Pat listens, without interrupting or defending Miss Jones, just saying at times 'Mmm... that sounds very difficult.' As Chloe pours out her woes, it becomes clearer that she has a lot of difficulty with maths, and is really floundering in that subject. Pat makes a mental note of this, and decides she will bring this up later with Chloe when she is calmer, when they might be able to discuss if there is any way of getting extra help with maths for Chloe.

PRESSING THE PAUSE BUTTON

The behaviour of teenagers can be very provocative, and it is perfectly normal to feel extreme anger towards them at such times. However, reacting with anger to a teenager's provocation is only likely to escalate the situation, and can lead to increasing verbal or physical aggression.

In the heat of the moment, it is easy to say or do things you later regret. Angry outbursts by parents or carers also run the risk of modelling this type of behaviour for the young person. So what can you do in the face of provocative, threatening or oppositional behaviour? 'Pressing the pause button' is a technique which helps you to remain in control, and gives you time to choose how you want to respond. It helps to defuse potentially volatile situations, and gives both you and the young person time to calm down. It does not mean ignoring issues that need to be addressed, but it does mean that this will be done at a time when you and the young person are calm and in the best state to address difficult issues.

AN EXAMPLE OF PRESSING THE PAUSE BUTTON

Brian and Moya are foster carers. Steve (14) has been in foster care with them for the past eight months. Things went smoothly for the first few months, but in recent weeks Steve has met up with new friends in the area, and things have not been going so well. The new friends are a bit older than Steve, and seem not to be in school, as Moya sees them hanging out in the local shopping centre during the day. Steve is supposed to be in at night by 10pm – this time has been worked out with him. In recent weeks he has been coming in later, and this has led to increasing conflict with Brian and Moya. One Saturday night he is particularly late. It is 11.30pm and he has not returned home. He is not responding to texts and calls from Brian to his mobile. Brian and Moya are becoming increasingly worried about him, and wonder if they should go out and search for him. At 11.45pm the doorbell rings. Brian answers it. It is Steve, looking dishevelled, smelling strongly of alcohol, swaying and slurring his words. Brian can feel a mixture of relief and anger welling up inside himself. He feels like hitting Steve, or at least giving him a good talking to. But he is a trained foster carer, and knows the best thing to do in situations like this is to 'press the pause button'. He takes a few deep breaths, helps Steve into the house, and says in a calm voice, 'You better go straight to bed. We will talk about this in the morning.'

This approach gives Brian and Moya time to decide how to respond. They know that Steve's behaviour needs to be addressed, and that there needs to be consequences for his staying out late and coming home drunk. They will talk this over tomorrow with him. They know this won't be easy, but they know it will be happening when they are calm, and Steve is sober.

CLEAR RULES, FEW RULES, CONSEQUENCES

Rules work best with young people if they are discussed with them, and if they have input into deciding what the consequences should be for breaking the rules. Families will have different views about what rules are most important, but in general it is better to have a small number of rules that are enforced, rather than many rules which are applied in a haphazard way. Most people would agree that basic rules covering safety and non-violence are essential. For young adolescents, this might include having a time to be home at night, knowing where they are and are not allowed to go, agreement that they will contact parents/carers if they are in difficulty, and no threatening or intimidating verbal or physical aggression. Agreeing in advance the consequences for breaking the rules helps to reduce conflict when they are actually broken. Parents are sometimes loath to involve adolescents in negotiations around consequences, as they fear they will be very lenient, but this is not usually the case. In deciding consequences, it is vital to choose something that can be enforced, and something that does not cause more problems for you as a parent or carer. For example, 'grounding' a young adolescent may be tolerable for you for one or two days, but longer periods of 'grounding' put more pressure on the adult than the adolescent, and are usually abandoned after a few days! Also, research has shown that short periods of grounding are as effective as long periods. Other consequences include loss of pocket money, coming in earlier, loss of access to a mobile phone or computer, additional chores, etc.

GIVING CHOICES

Rather than giving a blanket 'no', it is sometimes useful to give the young person a choice. This can help to avoid conflict, and can encourage the young person to take responsibility and make decisions. An example of where this approach might be used is the not uncommon situation in which a young person with repeated self-harm wants to remain home alone, but the parent knows that he is most likely to cut himself when at home alone. Giving a choice such as 'You can come with the rest of us on the family outing, or you can go to your gran's' may be useful, and may avert the inevitable conflict of an outright refusal to allow him to remain at home.

MEGAN'S CHOICE

Megan's mother decided to give her a choice, and told her she could go to the disco, but would be collected at midnight by herself or her dad. Megan rebelled against this idea, saying she would be mortified in front of her friends, and flounced out of the room, saying, 'If that's the case, I'm not going.' Megan's mother calmly said, 'It's your choice.'

A few hours later, Megan told her mother she had decided she would go, despite being collected. As it turned out, when collecting Megan, her dad was asked to give a lift home to two of her friends, and learned quite a lot about the disco from listening to their excited conversation in the back of the car!

Young people with DSH are no different from other young people in their need for boundaries and limits. Using some of the above ideas may help parents and carers to use discipline in a way which helps their young person to learn self-discipline, as he struggles to achieve independence and establish his own identity.

CHAPTER **7**

SPECIAL PROBLEMS

This chapter deals with particular problems which parents and carers may encounter in trying to help young people with DSH, such as self-harm and school, problems with friends/bullying, the child not accepting help, anger and aggression, child protection concerns, misuse of alcohol and drugs and the role of the internet and social networking sites.

SELF-HARM AND SCHOOL

A common concern is 'How much should we tell the school?' Young people usually do not want the school to know anything about their DSH, and will seek assurance that the school will not be told. This is a difficult situation, where the young person's right to confidentiality, but also her safety and wellbeing, have to be considered. There is no right or wrong way of dealing with it, as each young person's situation is different. In general, if you, as parent or carer, have concerns that your young person is self-harming or is vulnerable emotionally, it is usually in the best interest of the young person that someone who has responsibility in school for the young person should know of your concerns. This will enable them to 'keep an eye out' for the young person, to allow her to leave class without difficulty if she needs to attend appointments or just needs some time out, and may help avoid further stress for the young person. It may not be necessary to go into great detail about the nature of your concerns. Most school staff are very sensitive to the importance of young people not feeling they are in anyway 'different' in school, and are aware of the importance of discretion.

Young people with DSH are often struggling in school, academically or socially, or both. Parents or carers may be aware how stressful this is for the young person, but the school may not. The vast majority of schools encourage good communication with parents and carers, and things generally work out better for the young person where this is the case. Don't be afraid to seek a meeting with the Year Head or tutor to discuss how you can work together to reduce stress for your young person.

PROBLEMS WITH FRIENDS/BULLYING

Despite formal 'anti-bullying policies' in most schools and clubs, bullying is still very common. Sam describes below how he was bullied when he moved to a new school at the age of 11.

SAM'S STORY

When I was going into fifth class in primary school, I moved to a new school and for the first few months I was happy. It was a big change, but I thought my classmates seemed like nice guys and I thought that I'd get used to it. After a couple of months they turned nasty for no reason. The name-calling, the verbal abuse was the worst, but sometimes it got physical too – you know. The thing with bullies is that they go for people who either seem very quiet or very forward. Forward – as in they see you as a threat, and quiet – as in you're an easy victim. If you're in the middle they won't really go for you.

It started off very light, just the odd comment, but it got worse and worse. They'd always be looking for a fight. They thought they were hard men. They used to set people up to fight against each other. They did that to me. That was the only way to get their respect, to take on one of the big guys in the class and win. Someone would come up to me and say 'I heard what you said about me' and I wouldn't have said anything. Or they'd try to get me in trouble with the teachers. I think they might have bullied me because I was probably cleverer than they were. You had to act stupid; you had to act stupid, to be accepted because if you were clever they'd see you as an outsider. I had a different background too and I didn't fit in with their way of thinking.

I felt anxious, stressed and uptight about going to school. I'd do anything to get out of going. I pretended to be sick; I even made myself sick sometimes.

Bullying in adolescence is often so subtle that it may be difficult to recognize. Psychological bullying is just as hurtful and damaging as physical bullying – maybe even more so. It can take many forms, such as being excluded by a group, relentless 'slagging', having malicious rumours spread about you, receiving frightening or insulting texts, or having hurtful statements or photos posted on your Facebook page. Kevin describes how he was bullied at the age of 14.

KEVIN'S STORY

A few things happened at once. We moved house to a new area, and that was hard leaving my old friends and I had to change schools as well. This was in second year. After a short time in the new school I started getting slagged off and picked on. There would be ringleaders and when they would start then the rest would start too. The bullying can often be subtle, it could be guys picking on me in a jokey way or a sly punch or not being picked for the team in PE, but more serious stuff too, like being beaten up and verbal abuse.

They all had their established groups in the first year and they didn't want to let me in. At least that's what it felt like to me. At the lockers where we'd change our books at break time they'd ignore me. I wouldn't go down because I'd just be sitting there like a fool, doing nothing while they're all chatting away. Any time I'd try to join in they would tell me to shut up or get lost. It was harder at first because I knew no one in the school. I have some friends now so there are a few people who would stick up for me.

Being bullied can really affect you. I don't think the guys who were doing it to me realized just how much it bothered me. I would try not to show that I was getting upset but it was hard for me to hide it. Sometimes I would feel depressed about it and when I got home I'd just go up and sit in my room for ages and maybe cry sometimes, like just by myself.

Many young people who self-harm have experienced bullying. They are particularly vulnerable to being bullied because they may be perceived as being 'different' to peers, and may not have a supportive or protective group of friends. Being bullied often has a subtle effect on a person's self-esteem, leading them to believe that in some way they deserve to be bullied, and this is one of the reasons they find it so hard to tell anyone about it. Another reason they don't easily tell anyone is because they are afraid that adult intervention might make things worse.

You may suspect that bullying is happening, based on changes in your young person's behaviour – maybe reluctance to attend school or clubs, becoming increasingly withdrawn, or getting upset or angry after time spent on the internet or on her mobile phone. Directly asking if the young person is being bullied is likely to elicit a negative or hostile response. It may be better to be upfront about what you have noticed, saying something like 'I am a bit worried about you because I've noticed that you aren't going to your club any more, and you don't seem to be in good form. I'm wondering are you having hassle there?' This low-key approach may pave the way for your young person to talk to you about being bullied, although she is unlikely to use the term 'bullied'. Most young people who have experienced significant bullying say that telling someone what was happening was the first step in helping them to feel better about themselves. It is important to listen to them, to remain calm, and to work with them to plan how to address the problem.

You are likely to feel very upset and angry, knowing that your son or daughter is being bullied, but it is a good idea to give yourself a bit of time to 'cool off', and decide how best to proceed when you are calmer. Occasionally simple strategies can make a big difference, such as encouraging your young person to ignore the bullies, walk away, avoid being on her own, or making alternative arrangements for where she spends break and lunchtime. Knowing that she has your support can sometimes give that bit of extra confidence to the young person, which in some way reduces the bullying or its impact. If the bullying is more serious or persistent, it will need more active adult intervention. If it is happening in school, then the school needs to know, with details of what and who is involved. Your son or daughter is likely to resist this approach, but it needs to be considered when other approaches have failed. You can explain to your child that bullying occurs in every walk of life, and at every age, that it is not her fault, and that most people need help to get it sorted out. A meeting with the class tutor or Year Head is the place to start, making it clear that you want the bullying to stop, and asking how you and the school can work together to make that happen. If this does not work, the next port of call is a meeting with the Principal. If the bullying involves violence, or threats of violence, some parents report it to the police. Most schools take a proactive approach to dealing with bullying, but not all do. If the school is unable to stop the bullying, it may be in the young person's best interest to change schools, and in 'real life' this is often the decision made by parents and young people when bullying has been significant and impossible to eradicate.

'HE WON'T ACCEPT HELP'

Ideas for how to encourage a reluctant young person to attend for counselling or psychiatric treatment are discussed in Chapter 2. In practice, they work with most young people, but not with all. Most people are very frightened by the idea of 'having to see someone' about their problems, and young people are no different. Some young people with DSH are so depressed that they believe that nothing can help their situation, or that they deserve to feel the way they do.

How best to respond depends on how serious the problem is. In situations where there is an acute risk of suicide, it is essential that the young person gets help, and that a responsible adult remains with her until the appropriate help can be provided. This person is often a parent or carer, but may be a relative or trusted family friend. The presence of a calm, reassuring and trusted adult can often persuade a young person in acute distress to accept help.

It is very occasionally necessary to admit a young person involuntarily to a psychiatric hospital. This is reserved for situations where, because of a mental illness, there is a serious likelihood that the young person may cause immediate and serious harm to herself or to other people. The legislation governing involuntary admission, and its practical application, varies from country to country. In an emergency it is best to seek advice from your family doctor or local social services centre.

Less acute situations are much more common, where the young person may need specialist help, but there is no immediate threat to health or life. Such situations often involve young people who have become increasingly withdrawn and cut off from friends and family, and who may or may not be suicidal, but parents and carers usually fear that they are, particularly if they have self-harmed in the past. Such young people are often unable or unwilling to attend school or work, and spend most of the day in their rooms, often sleeping by day and emerging only at night when the rest of the family is in bed. It is often not clear if such young people are simply going through a particularly difficult adolescent phase, or whether they have an emerging serious mental health disorder.

It is worth discussing your concerns with your family doctor. If they know the young person, they may be able to advise, or may suggest that the young person attends for a check up. Your son or daughter may agree to this, and some family doctors are skilled in dealing with adolescent problems.

The involvement of both parents is generally helpful, even when they live apart. Many reluctant young people find it difficult to resist when parents present a united front in their attempts to get them to seek help. If referral to a mental health or counselling service is suggested, do attend, even if your young person refuses. You can discuss your concerns with the staff there, and some mental health services have outreach workers who will try to link up with the young person at home.

In the vast majority of situations, the young person eventually agrees to attend, or her situation improves with time. Sometimes the most you can do as a parent or carer is to keep some kind of communication open with your son or daughter until this happens.

ANGER AND AGGRESSION

DSH is sometimes described as anger directed towards oneself, but some young people who self-harm also direct their anger towards others, including parents and carers. Many parents of such young people tolerate angry and aggressive behaviour which they would not tolerate from anyone else, out of fear of making a bad situation worse. Chapter 6, 'Dealing with Discipline Issues' has some useful advice about deciding what to deal with, and what to let go, and how to manage your own anger, so as not to present an angry role model. 'Pressing the pause button' may help in situations in which tempers are rising, and may avoid escalations of aggressive behaviour. It is tempting, when things are calm, to avoid returning to the issue which sparked off the initial aggression, whether yours or hers, but it is better quietly to state the consequences when you are both calm, for example 'I am not sure how much it is going to cost to repair the door you damaged, but the cost will have to come out of your pocket money.'

Threats of physical aggression to you or another person are not unusual, and may involve the young person invading your body space, and 'shaping up' to you. Speaking calmly and assertively may lead to the young person backing off, but sometimes this is not enough, and it is safer to walk away. Serious physical aggression to family members should not be tolerated. In extreme cases it may be necessary to call the police and consider pressing charges, although this is easier said than done.

CHILD PROTECTION CONCERNS

You may have serious concerns about a young person, but not know what to do about them. For example, a teacher may have a student in her class who is self-harming, but whose parents have not responded to the school's requests that she seeks help. Or a youth worker or sports coach may have similar concerns. Organizations dealing with young people are required to have policies and procedures in place to handle child protection concerns, and there are clear pathways for dealing with such concerns. These usually involve discussion of the concerns with the line manager or designated child protection officer, who is required to report concerns to social services, who then carry out their own investigation. Some countries and states have mandatory reporting of child protection concerns, where there is a statutory obligation on professionals working with young people to report such concerns. Even where there is no mandatory reporting, it is best practice to report concerns, in order to protect children. Many countries have legislation to protect from being sued those who report child protection concerns in good faith. If you are working with young people, you should receive training and refresher courses in child protection.

The situation can be more difficult if you are a parent who has been told by your son or daughter about a friend who is self-harming or suicidal. You have no way of knowing who else knows, or if the young person is getting help. You may have been sworn to secrecy by your own son or daughter. There is no textbook way of dealing with this situation, but we all have a duty to protect young people and ensure that they get the help they need. If you are very good friends with the parents of the young person, you may share your concerns with them. Do not expect that they will thank you for doing this, as it is human nature to 'blame the messenger' who gives you unwelcome news. It may be necessary for you to pass on your concerns to the young person's school, or to social services if the school route is not possible. You can ask the school to keep your identity private, and reports to social services can be made anonymously. None of these are easy options, and before doing anything, it is a good idea to discuss the situation with someone you trust (you can do this without mentioning any names) to help you decide what is the best thing to do.

ALCOHOL AND DRUGS

There is a strong link between alcohol and drug misuse and DSH. Many studies have shown that alcohol plays a role in about 40 per cent of cases of DSH in young people, and alcohol misuse is also a risk factor for suicide. Alcohol reduces inhibitions as well as affecting mood, sometimes leading people to act on self-harming thoughts or suicidal acts when they would never have done so without alcohol. Binge drinking is extremely common in young people in Western cultures, and many parents and carers will have had the experience of their young teenage son or daughter arriving home drunk and disorientated. This is almost a rite of passage in Ireland, where excessive use of alcohol by people of all ages is a major problem. Many young people who self-harm repeatedly only do so when under the influence of alcohol.

When the young person's excessive drinking is becoming repeated and leading to other social, relationship, or family problems, intervention is needed. This can be very difficult, as the young person is likely to deny that her drinking is in any way causing problems, and may become angry and defensive when the subject is raised, leading people to 'back off', and so the cycle continues.

The relationship between the use of recreational drugs and DSH is similar to that with alcohol. The disinhibition caused by drug use, combined with the lowering of mood associated with coming down from a high, may lead to self-harm or even suicidal behaviour. People can react to drugs in unpredictable ways, sometimes leading to serious self-harm in people who have no history of DSH.

Some young people who are troubled by anxiety or depression or other mental health problems use alcohol or drugs as a type of medication to help them feel better. If you are concerned about a young person's alcohol or drug use, it is a good idea to seek out what services are available locally, and discuss your concerns with a professional who will be experienced in how best to facilitate a young person to get help. This can be a slow and difficult process, and parents and carers may need immense patience, as well as professional support, to help them keep channels of communication open, while waiting for the young person herself to acknowledge that she needs help.

THE INTERNET AND SOCIAL NETWORKING SITES

Using the internet and social networking sites can have many benefits, and it is an integral part of life for today's young people. The need for instant and continuous connection with others, known and unknown, can be hard for someone of my generation to understand, but I have learned from young people how much they value this, and what a central role it plays in their lives. The sense of connection with peers can have great benefits, particularly for socially anxious or withdrawn young people. The drawbacks include instant access to all sorts of information, all sorts of individuals, and the potential for cyberbullying, which is very common and involves offensive, abusive or degrading messages, comments, images or videos on social networking sites, by email or text.

The 'old-fashioned' advice to parents was to have the family computer located in the living room where you could keep an eye on what was being accessed, and to limit the young person's time on the computer. This advice is still appropriate for pre-teens, but is no longer practical where adolescents are concerned, many of whom have their own laptops or smart phones. Today's parents can best protect their young people from the negative aspects of the new technologies by trying to be as well informed as they can be (bearing in mind that young people will always be better informed!), having as good communication as possible with their young people, and knowing how to get information about what to do in cases of serious misuse of the internet.

The experts in social networking sites are your sons and daughters, and if you are curious about how they work, they may explain them to you, in a limited way! At least, having had such conversations, you will have some idea about what is involved, and may have opened up the possibility of them telling you if they are victims of cyberbullying. At our focus group meeting described in Chapter 8, parents and carers of young people who self-harm described how sometimes DSH was precipitated by cyberbullying. Research in this area has shown that cyberbullying is extremely common, and that most victims don't tell their parents for fear of their parents' over-reaction, or that their access to the internet might be stopped or limited. It has also been shown that it is very easy to be a cyberbully, without being aware that your behaviour constitutes cyberbullying.

If you are concerned that cyberbullying may be contributing to your young person's distress, try to talk to her about it. Mention what you have noticed, 'I notice you get very upset when you have been on the internet. Are you getting unpleasant messages?' She will almost certainly deny it initially, but if you are calm and matter of fact, she may tell you if it is happening. Try not to over-react. An acknowledgement of how hurtful it must be, and how you can understand her upset, is the best response initially. Later, when you are both calm, you can discuss how best to deal with it together. There is good information at www.reachout.com about dealing with cyberbullying. There is also much information on the internet about how to report or block offensive input to social networking sites or mobile phones, and how to get sites shut down. Parents have told me this is not as easy as it sounds, and needs much persistence. If you are an internet novice, ask a friend or colleague to help you with this process. Very occasionally it may be necessary to seek advice from the police in dealing with threatening messages.

The internet and social networking sites can be of great support to young people who are coping with DSH. Many useful websites are listed in the Appendix, some of which have video clips in which young people talk about what helped them through difficult times. Young people who refuse to attend counselling or mental health services may get support and good ideas from these.

CHAPTER **8**

PARENTS' AND PROFESSIONAL CARERS' VIEWS OF THEIR OWN SUPPORT NEEDS

This chapter provides an overview of a focus group meeting at which parents and carers of young people with self-harm or suicidal behaviour discussed their own support needs. The focus group was a very positive experience for the participants, who were able to discuss openly, sometimes for the first time, their sense of fear and isolation, and their need for support in communicating with their young person, handling further threats or episodes of self-harm, dealing with everyday discipline issues, and re-establishing family life.

Teachers' support needs are also discussed and include having a place to discuss concerns, managing issues relating to confidentiality, and how best to provide support within the boundary of the teacher–student relationship.

There is very little research on the effects of self-harm by young people on those who care for them and about them. A research study carried out in 2006 by Raphael and colleagues involved in-depth face-to-face interviews with parents of young people who had self-harmed (Raphael, Clarke and Kumar 2006). These parents reported that self-harm by their son/daughter was extremely traumatic for them, leading to feelings of helplessness and concerns about their ability to cope as parents when their young person was discharged from hospital. Some parents reported that the information and support provided by professionals was very inadequate, and that with more support, they felt they would have been better able to help their young people through their difficulties. Another study, carried out in 2000 by Wagner and colleagues, investigated parents' emotional and behavioural responses to adolescents' suicide attempts (Wagner *et al.* 2000). Parents were interviewed soon after the event using both open-ended and structured interviews. Mothers' reactions included an increase in sad, caring and anxious feelings, with approximately half feeling angry and hostile after the suicide attempt. However, few verbalized these feelings and many reported being careful about what they said following the suicide attempt. The authors suggested that therapeutic work with parents should focus on helping them to realize how normal their feelings were, and should provide help with family communication skills.

FOCUS GROUP MEETING

The DSH Team in Children's University Hospital, Dublin involves nurses, psychiatrists and social workers whose job is to assess young people who present to the accident and emergency department with self-harm or suicidal behaviour. They have carried out over one thousand such assessments in the past ten years, and are very aware of the huge stress on families and carers of young people who self-harm. They are also aware of the crucial role families and carers play in supporting these young people.

In 2006 the team decided to seek the views of parents and carers about their own support needs, and to ask them if a support programme for parents and carers would be a good idea. They thought that the best people to provide this information would be people who were living with the problem of self-harm in young people. The team contacted all the parents and carers of young people who had attended the hospital accident and emergency department over the previous three years, to invite them to attend a focus group meeting to discuss the setting up of a support group which would be specific for their needs. They also asked the local CAMHS and family support agencies to notify parents and carers of the meeting.

The meeting was held in the hospital and was attended by 15 parents and 10 childcare staff working in residential children's homes. The DSH Team welcomed the participants, gave them background information about how common self-harm and suicidal behaviour are in young people, and how many parents had asked for additional support. They were asked, as the experts in what supports were needed by parents/carers of young people who had engaged in self-harm, to tell us if our idea of a support group for parents was useful, and what should be involved in such a group.

The 25 participants were divided into five subgroups, each subgroup being led by one member of the DSH Team who acted as a facilitator. Two key questions, chosen prior to the meeting, were asked of each group. These questions allowed for open-ended discussion:

- What areas do you think a support group should address?

- What would you like to gain and/or learn from participating in such a support group?

The subgroups discussed the above topics for 45 minutes, following which each facilitator summarized the group's discussion content with the participants. The whole group then reconvened and summaries from each of the subgroups were presented. Findings were consolidated and time was given for any additional discussion. After the meeting the participants completed a feedback form asking about their experience of the meeting. They gave us permission to use their experiences and quotations anonymously for education and to support service development.

A professional stenographer recorded the contents of the discussion, and the researchers then analyzed these recordings to determine the themes which had been discussed. The following were the main themes:

- Support
- Emotions
- Parenting difficulties
- Family
- Information
- Management of episodes of self-harm
- School
- Internet.

Support

This included the lack of support from services, the need for support for parents and carers, and the benefits of support from other people in the same situation.

> *'When I left A&E I felt I had nowhere to go… I had no idea as to what to do, where to go, how to get help.'*

'Once I left that hour of therapy I had nothing...no background support.'

'That [support] would be the one thing I feel would be a real benefit of coming to a group like this.'

'...if there was one thing this group [programme] could provide, it's support.'

'It would be a relief to be able to talk to someone else who has gone through it.'

'Knowing other people having the same situation really does help.'

'...the relief of knowing I'm not the only one.'

'Attending today has really helped, to look at other parents and say "God, they're just like me, they are all good and normal and ordinary."'

Emotions

Participants described a range of emotions including guilt, fear, frustration, isolation and a lack of self-confidence following their child's self-harm.

'The first thing you do as a parent is blame yourself.'

'...feeling guilty – is it my fault?'

'The guilt...that's the hard thing to deal with.'

'...feeling you're no good as a parent...a failing.'

'Where did I fail?... You can't protect her from the outside world, you just can't.'

'I remember the panic waiting for an appointment.'

'The whole thing is really, really scary.'

'...angry towards her.'

'How dare she...it's upsetting the whole household.'

'She's good at making you feel guilty.'

'You go around trying to cover up, not discussing it in front of family or friends.'

'The biggest thing is the isolation, terror and fear...it's a very harsh journey.'

Parenting difficulties

Parents questioned their confidence in parenting their young people, and their ability to communicate with them.

'...to gain confidence in dealing with this...'

'Your trust is gone and it's difficult to build that up with them again.'

'...retain what you had before.'

'...how to help us to open up and to get in touch with the anger, but express it...'

'...how to parent a teenager because I don't have a clue.'

'How do I discipline...manage manipulative behaviour?'

'What limits should we set on them?... I tend to give in to him now.'

Family

The impact of DSH on the whole family was a major theme. Parents worried about how to explain to siblings and respond to their needs at a time when the young person who self-harmed was the main focus of parents' attention. They felt that the whole dynamic of family life was affected.

'...terrible problem is how to deal with siblings...what to tell them...'

'It's almost as if the rest of the family doesn't matter...'

'...it becomes the centre of the family and the whole dynamic breaks down and it's all about this one person...'

'How do we get back to being a normal family?'

'...learn how to balance the situation, so that the whole world doesn't revolve around her.'

'...it's so unfair to his sister and us...his sister can't cope with it.'

Information

Young people's mental health, reasons why young people self-harm, and information about treatment services were of keen interest to participants. Such information was considered important to managing and preventing further self-harm.

'I think a discussion around why do young people self-harm would be useful and ways in which to prevent it in the first place...'

'If you have the knowledge and background you feel more confident in dealing with it.'

Management of episodes of self-harm

Advice on how to prevent, or manage further threats/ episodes of self-harm was seen as a priority. Carers were especially concerned about the potential for contagion effects in residential care home setting. Case examples were suggested as being a useful means to learning the above.

'...what triggers to be aware of.'

'Some of it is attention seeking...not sure how to react.'

'...when to intervene...take precautions'.

School

Participants described a lack of support and understanding from schools, and many were reluctant to inform schools of the problem.

'I feel I should tell the school, but I'm not sure.'

'How can my child deal with slagging from other people in school...what advice can I give him?'

Internet

Parents made an association between DSH and internet use, feeling it directly influenced their child's behaviour.

'She's on the net where there is an awful lot of bullying going on...it's another place they can be targeted...'

'Most times she cuts is after being on the internet – it seems to be caused by remarks on the net...'

SPACE PROGRAMME

The participants who attended this meeting gave very positive feedback about it, and the atmosphere of the meeting was extremely supportive. This was a surprise to the DSH Team, who had anticipated that the issue of lack of services might predominate, with anger and frustration being the main themes. It seemed that the opportunity to meet other parents and carers 'in the same boat' was of great benefit to both parents and childcare staff. Parents also said how much comfort they got from hearing that even professional childcare staff found DSH hard to cope with, while the childcare staff were able to empathize with the struggles of parents, and remarked that 'at least we can switch off when our shift is over'.

This meeting led to the development of the SPACE programme, an eight-week group support programme for parents and carers of young people with DSH. SPACE stands for Supporting Parents and Carers of young people with self-harm or suicidal behaviour. The programme is run three times a year by the DSH Team of Children's University Hospital, Dublin and is available without referral or charge to any parent or carer of a young person under 18 years, where there is concern about self-harm or suicidal behaviour. It is run in a city centre hotel in Dublin, which is very convenient for public transport, and is run in the evenings to facilitate as many parents and carers as possible to attend. The main aims of the programme are to provide what parents and carers told us they want, namely support, along with information about DSH and mental health problems in young people, and help with parenting adolescents and communication skills. There is a big emphasis in the programme on the importance of 'looking after yourself' as a parent or carer, as this can be a long and difficult journey. The programme has been run now with over 300 parents and carers, and the preliminary evaluation has been very positive. It is now being evaluated using a randomized controlled trial. The description of the meeting described above which led to the development of the SPACE programme, and the results of its preliminary evaluation have been published (Byrne *et al.* 2008; Power *et al.* 2009).

SUPPORT NEEDS OF TEACHERS

There are even fewer studies which have looked at the support needs of teachers, but through working with teachers for many years, I know they have support needs in relation to DSH which are often unrecognized and unspoken. Many teachers have told me how common DSH is among the students they teach, of their confusion about how to respond when they suspect one of their students has a problem with DSH, of their lack of training on issues relating to mental health in young people, and of their school's lack of an official policy on how to respond to a young person with this type of difficulty.

Teachers in general want to support a student with DSH, but are aware of the need to do this within the bounds of the teacher–student relationship. They recognize that they are not carers, counsellors or therapists. Nonetheless, teachers often spend more time than any of these in direct contact with such young people. They need to be working in a situation where it is possible to discuss their concerns with a more senior colleague, school counsellor or school psychologist, where there are clear policies on confidentiality and notification of parents or guardians, where child protection protocols are clear to all and are followed, and where the ethos of the school is supportive to students and staff alike.

Useful information for teachers on DSH and how to respond is thin on the ground, but there is a useful online resource at www.educatorsandselfinjury.com, which describes itself as 'the missing manual to understanding and dealing with students who self injure', by Laura A. Dorko, a school psychologist in the USA. This manual deals specifically with self-injury, but the principles it outlines apply to other forms of DSH. It gives information on how to recognize self-injury, acknowledging that it is not uncommon to feel shocked or even repulsed by it. It stresses the importance of a calm, understanding approach. It cautions against ignoring DSH, stressing the important role teachers may have in ensuring that the young person gets the help he needs. This will involve liaison with the school counsellor, and following the school's protocol on linking with parents with a view to referral to the appropriate service.

Except in crisis situations, which are thankfully uncommon, teachers rarely have to act immediately to concerns about a student who may be self-harming. There is usually time to discuss concerns with a colleague, or to seek advice from a mental health professional, so that a planned approach can be taken to ensure that the student gets appropriate help.

CHAPTER **9**

SELF-HARM
WHAT DOES THE FUTURE HOLD?

Will my son/daughter always be prone to self-harm? Is there a risk of suicide? Can suicide be prevented? Is there anything parents and carers can do to reduce the risk? Will my young person be alright in adulthood? These are some of the questions this chapter attempts to answer.

Most parents and carers of young people with DSH have considerable concerns for the future. Will their young people continue to self-harm into adulthood? Will they develop mental health disorders as they get older? Can DSH lead to death by suicide? Will they be able to form adult relationships and lead healthy, productive lives?

Research in this area is quite limited, because very few studies have followed up young people with DSH from adolescence into adult life. To do such studies properly is time-consuming and expensive, but such a study has recently been done in Australia (Moran *et al.* 2011). This study selected a random sample of almost 2000 young people attending schools across the state of Victoria, and interviewed them at regular intervals between the ages of 15 and 29. Eight per cent of the young people reported

DSH in adolescence, but over 90 per cent of these reported no DSH in early adulthood, when DSH was much less common. Young women were somewhat more likely than young men to report DSH in adolescence, and were more likely to continue to self-harm into adulthood. Less than 1 per cent of the young people who reported DSH said it was associated with suicidal intent. Adolescents who reported DSH were more likely to have symptoms of depression and anxiety, anti-social behaviour, misuse of alcohol, and use of cannabis, and there was an association between having those problems in adolescence and reporting DSH in early adulthood.

The results of this study are very encouraging for parents and carers. They show that DSH does not continue into adulthood in most young people, and suggest a number of reasons why this might be the case. Important biological changes occur in the brain as young people mature, perhaps leading them to have better emotional control. Also, as they enter adult life, they may become more independent, and therefore better able to cope with family and peer stresses. Unfortunately, studies of this type cannot tell us which individual young person will continue to self-harm, but the study suggests that treatment of depression, anxiety, anti-social behaviour and excessive use of alcohol in adolescence may result in less DSH in adult life.

IS THERE A RISK OF SUICIDE?

Many studies have shown a link between DSH and death by suicide, but it is important to remember that DSH is very common, while death by suicide is much rarer. The risk is highest in that small group of young people who begin self-harming in adolescence and continue to do so into adult life, often with increasingly serious types of self-harm and with increasing suicidal intent. These young people have often had very traumatic life experiences, and are very difficult to engage in services. Many forms of conventional treatment do not seem to help them. Follow-up studies of this group have shown that their death rates from suicide and other 'non-natural' causes are higher than in the general population, but in most cases their self-harming behaviour tends to reduce as they get older. Dialectic behaviour therapy (see p.35) has been shown to be of value to some of them, helping them to manage their difficulties in a healthier way.

CAN SUICIDE BE PREVENTED?

It is probably true to say that suicide cannot be prevented in someone who is absolutely determined to end her life in this way. However, such determination is rare, and tends to wax and wane, depending on many other factors affecting the person's life. These factors include having a mental health disorder such as depression or psychosis, misusing alcohol or drugs, being socially isolated, having made previous suicide attempts, and having relationship difficulties. While most DSH is not suicidal in intent, some self-harm acts are true suicide attempts, and it can be difficult even for experienced mental health professionals to be clear which is the case. If you, as a parent or carer, have concerns that your young person is suicidal, please see Chapter 2 for advice on practical steps to take to reduce the risk and ensure that your young person gets the necessary professional help.

HOW CAN PARENTS/CARERS HELP?

The fact that you have read this book this far shows your commitment to helping your young person towards a healthy and independent adult life in which she will be able to achieve her potential and form good relationships. The book outlines the importance of the support you provide by keeping communication going, giving positive attention, taking steps to reduce family conflict and stress, and getting professional help for your young person, and support for yourself when this is needed. You need to look after yourself by building into your routine some time just for you, doing something to keep your batteries charged, whether it is something physical like going to the gym, or mental, like learning a new skill, or social, like keeping up with friends (see pp.54–55). This is so easy to advise, but so hard to do when you are immersed in the demands of coping with a young person with DSH. It is important because you need to keep yourself as well and strong as you can, to be able to provide the support your young person needs. But it also conveys without words a strong message of hope to your young person, that life is worth living.

BECKY'S STORY

Becky is 21 and training to be a healthcare assistant. Her parents are very proud of her, as they know what a difficult time she has been through. There were times when she was a teenager when they feared she might never reach her twenties. She is now living away from home sharing a flat with three other girls, and studying a course in which she is really interested. She is full of life and fun, and her parents feel they are very lucky. They sometimes wonder what made the difference for Becky, what helped her to come through depression and self-harm in her teens. They never consider how their own support played a vital role in this.

Becky is their youngest child. She seemed happy, confident and outgoing as a small child, but never really enjoyed school, as she found reading and maths quite difficult. She was assessed because of her reading difficulty in primary school, and her parents were told she did not have dyslexia, but was just a bit behind in her reading. They helped her with this as much as they could, and she managed to scrape by in primary school.

Things started to go wrong in the first year in secondary school. Becky found it very hard to settle in, did not seem to have much in common with the other girls, and found the work really difficult. By the second year, when she was 14, she was truanting from school and hanging out with a group of older friends, most of whom were also truanting. At home she was angry and abusive, and it was almost impossible to have any sort of conversation with her. Her parents had very different views about what was going on for her. Her mother felt she was troubled and needed understanding and patience, while her father and older brother and sister felt she was 'a spoilt brat'. There was huge conflict in the family. After a particularly bitter row, Becky scratched her forearm with a broken picture frame. The cuts were very superficial, but her parents were horrified – this was something they had never encountered before. Becky's mother brought her to the family doctor, who spoke with the two of them together first, and then spoke with Becky on her own. The doctor said he wanted to refer Becky to the local CAMHS, but she refused to go, saying she was fine, and her parents needed to 'lighten up'.

Things did not get any easier over the following year. Becky rarely went to school, and when she was 15, she announced that she was leaving school. By then she was in a relationship with a boy who was much older than her, leading to more conflict at home. Becky continued to cut herself after rows. She thought her parents did not know about this, as she was careful to wear long-sleeved tee shirts, but her mother had seen spots of blood on her duvet cover, and suspected she was still self-harming. Her parents knew she needed help, but felt powerless, as she refused to attend any service.

Following the breakup of her relationship with her boyfriend, Becky took a serious overdose of paracetamol, and spent three days in hospital, as there was concern that she might have liver damage. She was assessed by the mental health team while in hospital, who suggested that she attend the local CAMHS following discharge. The nurse on the mental health team met with Becky every day when she was in hospital, and Becky got on well with her. To her parents' amazement and relief, she agreed to attend for follow-up help. Her parents will never forget the day she was discharged from hospital after her overdose. They were terrified she would take another overdose if things were not going well for her. The appointment with the CAMHS was for the following week, and they felt as if they were 'walking on egg shells' as they waited for the appointment.

Both parents went with Becky to her first appointment, and to their immense relief, it went well. Becky saw a therapist, and her parents met with another therapist who listened to their concerns, and seemed to understand their mixed feelings of concern for Becky, but also anger at what she had done, and all they had been through. Her parents were told that Becky was depressed, and that her behaviour problems were related to this. Through working with their own therapist, they learned the importance of not getting sucked into rows, with Becky and with each other. They attended a course for parents of young people with behavioural and emotional difficulties, where they learned a lot, both from the course but also from the other parents. They started to feel a bit better about themselves, and more confident that they could make a difference to their family life using some of the ideas they learned on the course. Meanwhile Becky was having weekly sessions with her therapist. She did not talk about these, but the very fact that she was attending was a comfort to her parents. Sometimes they had joint sessions, when Becky and her therapist met with her parents and their therapist. Through these they learned of Becky's despair at times, of her feelings of inadequacy and failure as she compared herself to her older brother and sister, both of whom had done well at school and now had good jobs and were in stable relationships. Communication between them started to improve.

They attended the service on and off over a two-year period, during which things gradually seemed to get better. With the support of her therapist, Becky enrolled in an early school leavers programme, and seemed to get a lot out of this, as it concentrated on practical and technical skills, which made sense to Becky in a way which school work never had. She finished the course when she was 18 and was unemployed for a few months, but then got a job as a junior in a hairdressers. This went alright for a while, but Becky realized that she wanted to work as a healthcare assistant. She hoped this might lead on to training in youth work or care of young people with difficulties, because, as she put it, 'I know what it's like to feel crap.'

Becky was discharged from the mental health service when she was 18, having had no further episodes of DSH for the previous year. Through the sessions with her therapist, she had learned to manage the times she felt down, when the urge to self-harm sometimes came back. She would distract herself by doing some of the relaxation exercises she had learned, or phoning a friend. Her parents were nervous as the time for her discharge drew near, but their fears have gradually lessened as the years since then have passed.

Becky's parents feel they have all been changed by the experience they have been through. They value 'ordinary life' in a way they never did before. They see that Becky's older brother and sister are more tolerant and less judgemental, and it gives them great joy to see Becky becoming a more confident young woman, with clear hopes and plans for her future. If you asked them what had helped Becky, they might say it was the nurse in the hospital who persuaded her to get help for herself, or the therapist who got on so well with her, or the teachers in the early school leavers programme whose confidence in Becky gave her a sense of achievement. All those people played a part, but what about their own role? They probably would not recognize how important their support was in helping Becky, their 'being there' for her, encouraging her, and keeping hope alive. They would not mention this, though it may have been the most important factor in helping Becky through her 'tough times'.

You cannot 'cure' your young person of DSH, she needs to do that for herself, but your support and understanding as she makes that journey can be invaluable. There is an old Irish saying *go n-éirigh an bóthar leat*, which means 'may the road rise with you'. It is a particularly suitable wish for young people who self-harm, and for those who care for them and about them. The road is often steep, and may be long, but even the longest, steepest road levels off eventually. The support of those they meet along the way, and who walk the road with them, can make a huge difference to these young people, acknowledging their struggle and keeping hope alive. I hope this book helps you on your journey.

APPENDIX

RESOURCES

RESOURCES IN YOUR COMMUNITY

- Family and friends
- Your child's school counsellor
- Your family doctor, who may be able to help directly, or may advise on local counselling or mental health services for young people
- The young person's social worker, if he has one
- In a crisis, the local hospital accident and emergency department.

USEFUL BOOKS

McDougall, T., Armstrong, M. and Trainor, G. (2010) *Helping Children and Young People Who Self-harm.* Oxford: Routledge.

This easy-to-read book, written by three consultant mental health nurses with much experience of the area, is primarily for professionals, but also contains information of interest to the general reader.

Freeman, J. (2010) *Cover Up: Understanding Self-Harm.* Dublin: Veritas.

Written for the general reader, parents, teachers and therapists, this useful book explains self-harm and suicidal behaviour, and describes the admirable treatment approach provided by Pieta House in Ireland.

Hawton, K., Rodham, K. and Evans, E. (2006) *By Their Own Young Hand: Deliberate Self-harm and Suicidal Ideas in Adolescents.* London: Jessica Kingsley Publishers.

This easy-to-read book is written mainly for professionals, and may be of particular interest to teachers, as it reports a study conducted with schools in the UK, looking at the prevalence of deliberate self-harm in the community.

Levenkron, S. (1998) *Cutting: Understanding and Overcoming Self-Mutilation.* New York: W.W. Norton and Company.

Written for 'self-mutilators, parents, friends, therapists' – this book explains self-cutting, how it develops, and how it can be helped. It has an easy-to-read style, and is engaging. Although it is limited to self-cutting, much of it is relevant to those caring for young people who engage in other forms of self-harm, such as overdoses.

Shamoo, T.K. and Patros, P.G. (1990) *Helping Your Child Cope with Depression and Suicidal Thoughts.* San Francisco, CA: Jossey-Bass.

There is much useful information in this book, which has stood the test of time, and is of particular relevance to parents and carers in the USA.

USEFUL ORGANISATIONS

Samaritans: A 24-hour service offering confidential support to anyone who is in a crisis.

Telephone Helpline UK: 08457 90 90 90

Telephone Helpline Ireland: 1850 60 90 90

Telephone Helpline USA: 1 (800) 273-TALK

Telephone Helpline Australia: 08 9381 55 55

Befrienders Worldwide with Samaritans gives contact details for helplines in many countries throughout the world through it's website, www.befrienders.org.

YoungMinds: A UK-based charity committed to improving the mental health of all young people. It runs a parents' helpline which offers free, confidential online and telephone support and advice to any adult with concerns about the mental health of a young person up to the age of 25 years. Tel: 0808 802 5544; email: parents@youngminds.org.uk.

USEFUL WEBSITES

www.rcpsych.ac.uk/mentalhealthinfo/mentalhealthand-growingup.aspx

Website of the Royal College of Psychiatrists in the UK. Information for parents, carers and young people about a range of issues including self-harm in young people.

www.helpguide.org/mental/self_injury.htm

USA website with universal relevance. Includes many suggestions of alternative ways of coping with overwhelming feelings. Has a section on helping a family member.

www.reachout.com

Interactive and informative Australian website for young people, with convincing video clips made by real young people about how they coped with suicidal thoughts, depression, self-harm and many other difficulties.

www.mind.org.uk

Website of a UK mental health charity. Has informative sections on self-harm, suicidal thoughts, and how to support a family member or friend.

www.aacap.org

Website of the American Academy of Child and Adolescent Psychiatry. Click onto Facts for Families. Useful information on self-injury, and suicide.

www.youngminds.org.uk

Website of a UK-based charity committed to improving the mental health of all young people. Good advice for parents and carers about how to help and how to access services in the UK.

www.teenagehealthfreak.org

Aimed at young people, has very user-friendly advice on suicidal thoughts and self-harm.

www.educatorsandselfinjury.com

For school staff. Describes itself as 'the missing manual to understanding and dealing with students who self-injure.' Further information about the content is on p.89.

www.decd.sa.gov.au

Website of the South Australian Department for Education and Child Development. Enter 'self harm' into the search engine on the home page to access an excellent booklet entitled 'An information booklet for young people who self harm and those who care for them'.

www.spunout.ie

Informative website dealing with many issues affecting young people. Includes a wide-ranging guide to mental health services in Ireland.

www.headspace.org.au

The National Youth Mental Foundation in Australia offers support to young people aged 12 to 25 and their parents/carers. It operates centres throughout Australia.

www.suicidepreventionlifeline.org

The National Suicide Prevention lifeline's mission is to provide immediate assistance to individuals in suicidal crisis in the USA by connecting them to the nearest available suicide prevention and mental health service provider through a toll-free telephone number: 1-800-273-TALK (8255). It is the only national suicide prevention and intervention telephone resource funded by the USA Federal Government.

REFERENCES

Byrne, S., Morgan, S., Fitzpatrick, C., Boylan, C. *et al.* (2008) 'Deliberate self-harm in children and adolescents: A qualitative study exploring the needs of parents and carers.' *Clinical Child Psychology and Psychiatry 13,* 493–504.

Connor, J.J. and Rueter, M.A. (2006) 'Parent–child relationships as systems of support or risk for adolescent suicidality.' *Journal of Family Psychology 20,* 143–155.

Cooper, J., Kapur, N., Webb, R., Lawlor, M. *et al.* (2005) 'Suicide after deliberate self harm.' *American Journal of Psychiatry 162,* 297–303

Green, J.M., Wood, A.J., Kerfoot, M.J., Trainor, G. *et al.* (2011) 'Group therapy for adolescents with repeated self-harm: Randomised controlled trial with economic evaluation.' *British Medical Journal 342,* available online.

Harrington, R., Pickles, A., Aglan, A., Harrington, V., Burroughs, H. and Kerfoot, M. (2006) 'Early adult outcomes of adolescents who deliberatley poisned themselves.' *Journal of the American Academy of Child and Adolescent Psychiatry 45,* 337–345.

Hawton, K.K.E., Houston, K. and Shepperd, R. (1999) 'Suicide in young people – Study of 174 cases, aged under 25 years, based on coroners' and medical records.' *British Journal of Psychiatry 175,* 271–276.

Hawton, K.K.E, Rodham, K., Evans, E. and Weatherall, R. (2002) 'Deliberate self harm in adolescents: Self report survey in schools in England.' *British Medical Journal 325,* 1207–1211.

Hawton, K.K.E., Townsend, E., Arensman, E., Gunnell, D. *et al.* (1999) 'Psychosocial and pharmacological treatments for deliberate self-harm.' *Cochrane Database of Systematic Reviews 4,* CD001764.

Hawton, K., Rodham, K., Evans, E. and Weatherall, R. (2002) 'Deliberate self harm in adolescents: Self report survey in schools in England.' *British Medical Journal 325,* 1207–1211.

McLean, J., Maxwell, M., Platt, S., Harris, F. and Jepson, R. (2008) *Risk and Protective Factors for Suicide and Suicidal Behaviour: A Literature Review.* Edinburgh: Scottish Government Social Research. Available at www.Scotland.gov.uk/Publications/2008/11/28141444/23

Messer, S.B. and Wampold, B.E. (2002) 'Let's face facts: Common factors are more potent than specific therapy ingredients.' *Clinical Psychology: Science and Practice 9*, 21–25.

Moran, P., Coffey, C., Romaniuk, H., Olsson, C. *et al.* (2011) 'The natural history of self-harm from adolescence to young adulthood: A population-based cohort study.' *The Lancet 379*, 9812, 236–243.

NICE (National Institute for Clinical Excellence) (2004) *Self-harm: Short-term Treatment and Management.* London: NICE. Available at www.nice.org.uk/nicemedia/live/10946/29425/29425.pdf

Power, L., Morgan, S., Byrne, S., Boylan, C. *et al.* (2009) 'A pilot study evaluating a support programme for parents of young people with suicidal behaviour.' *Child and Adolescent Psychiatry and Mental Health 3*, 20. Available at www.nccbi.nlm.nih.gov/pmc articles/PMC271705

Raphael, H., Clarke, G. and Kumar, S. (2006) 'Exploring parents' responses to their child's deliberate self-harm.' *Health Education Journal 106*, 9–20.

Shaffer, D., Gould, M.S., Fisher, P., Trautman, P. *et al.* (1996) 'Psychiatric diagnosis in child and adolescent suicide.' *Archives of General Psychiatry 53*, 339–348.

Sullivan, C., Arensman, E., Keeley, H., Corcoran, P. and Perry, I.J. (2004) *Young People's Mental Health: A Report of the Results from the Lifestyle and Coping Survey.* Cork: National Suicide Research Foundation.

Wagner, B.M., Aiken, C., Mullaley, P.M. and Tobin, J.J. (2000) 'Parent's reactions to adolescents' suicide attempts.' *Journal of the American Academy of Child and Adolescent Psychiatry 39*, 429–436.

Wood, A., Trainor, G., Rothwell, J., Moore, A. and Harrington, R.C. (2001) 'Randomized trial of group therapy for repeated deliberate self-harm in adolescents.' *Journal of the American Academy of Child and Adolescent Psychiatry 40*, 1246–1253.

INDEX

A Short Introduction to Promoting Resilience in Children

Colby Pearce
Paperback: £12.99/$19.95
ISBN: 978-1-84905-118-7
112 pages

A child's capacity to cope with adversity and 'stand on their own two feet' is seen as critical to their development, well-being, and future independence and success in adulthood. Psychological strength, or resilience, directly affects a child's capacity to cope with adversity.

This book provides a succinct, accessible and clear guide on how to promote resilience in children and achieve positive developmental outcomes for them. The author covers three key factors that affect resiliency: vulnerability to stress and anxiety, attachment relationships and access to basic needs. For each, the author presents practical advice and strategies, such as how to regulate children's stress and anxiety, how to encourage and maintain secure attachments, and how to assure children that their needs are understood and will be met. The model presented will help parents and carers ensure their children grow up happy, healthy and resilient.

This book will be invaluable for parents, carers and practitioners in supportive roles caring for children.

Colby Pearce is Principal Psychologist at Secure Start, a private psychology practice based in Adelaide, Australia, that specializes in service provision to children and adolescents who have experienced complex trauma. He is the author of *A Short Introduction to Attachment and Attachment Disorder* and has extensive experience in teaching and training of psychologists and other professionals who work with children.

A Short Introduction to Attachment and Attachment Disorder

Colby Pearce
Paperback: £12.99/$20.95
ISBN: 978-1-84310-957-0
112 pages

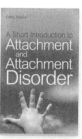

This book presents a short and accessible introduction to what 'attachment' means and how to recognize attachment disorders in children.

The author explains how complex problems in childhood may stem from the parent–child relationship during a child's early formative years, and later from the child's engagement with the broader social world. It explores the mindset of difficult and traumatized children and the motivations behind their apparently antisocial and defensive tendencies.

A Short Introduction to Attachment and Attachment Disorder includes case vignettes to illustrate examples, and offers a comprehensive set of tried-and-tested practical strategies for parents, carers and practitioners in supportive roles caring for children.

**Responding to Self-Harm in
Children and Adolescents
A Professional's Guide to Identification,
Intervention and Support**
Steven Walker
Paperback: £15.99/$27.95
ISBN: 978-1-84905-172-9
144 pages

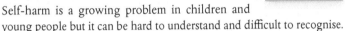

Self-harm is a growing problem in children and
young people but it can be hard to understand and difficult to recognise.

Responding to Self-Harm in Children and Adolescents will help
professionals to understand self-harm and respond appropriately. It
covers what the risk factors are, including social exclusion, and who
is most likely to self-harm. Information on what self-harm is and
what causes it, including mental health issues, problems in childhood
and trauma, is included. The book also covers how to recognise self-
harm and how to immediately respond in an emergency, and different
intervention methods are explored. Finally, the author discusses means
of support, including how parents and friends can help.

This accessible guide provides clear and easily digestible
information and practical advice to any professional working with a
child or young person who is suspected of, or actually self-harming.

Steven Walker is Head of Child and Adolescent Mental Health at Anglia
Ruskin University, UK. He is a registered social worker and psychotherapist
and has worked in social care for over 30 years, specialising in child protection
and child and adolescent mental health.

By Their Own Young Hand
Deliberate Self-harm and Suicidal Ideas in Adolescents

Keith Hawton and Karen Rodham
With Emma Evans
Paperback: £19.99/$35.95
ISBN: 978-1-84310-230-4
264 pages

Self-harm in adolescents is an increasingly recognised problem, and there is growing awareness of the important role schools and health services can play in detecting and supporting those at risk. *By Their Own Young Hand* explores the findings of the first large-scale survey of deliberate self-harm and suicidal thinking in adolescents in the UK, and draws out the implications for prevention strategies and mental health promotion.

Six thousand young people were asked about their experiences of self-harm, the coping methods they use, and their attitudes to the help and support available. The authors identify the risk and protective factors for self-harm, exploring why some adolescents with suicidal thoughts go on to harm themselves while others do not, what motivates some young people to seek help and whether distressed teenagers feel they receive the support they need. *By Their Own Young Hand* offers practical advice on how schools can detect young people at risk, cope with the aftermath of self-harm or attempted suicide and develop training programmes for teachers. It also examines the roles of self-help, telephone helplines, email counselling and walk-in crisis centres.

Packed with adolescents' own personal accounts and perspectives, this accessible overview will be essential reading for teachers, social workers and mental health professionals.

Keith Hawton is Professor of Psychiatry and Director of the Centre for Suicide Research at the University of Oxford. He is co-editor of the *International Handbook of Suicide and Attempted Suicide*, co-author of *Deliberate Self-harm in Adolescence*, also published by Jessica Kingsley Publishers, and has been presented with awards from the International Association for Suicide Prevention (1995), the American Association of Suicidology (2001) and the American Foundation for Suicide Prevention (2002). **Karen Rodham** is a Research Fellow at the Centre for Suicide Research at the University of Oxford, focusing on the lifestyle and coping skills of adolescents. **Emma Evans** is a Research Assistant at the Centre for Suicide Research at the University of Oxford, and has also undertaken research into effective provision of preschool education.

Deliberate Self-Harm in Adolescence
Claudine Fox and Keith Hawton
Child and Adolescent Mental Health series
Paperback: £17.99/$32.95
ISBN: 978-1-84310-237-3
144 pages

Self-harm in adolescence and late teens is known to be increasing, though it is difficult to detect and inconsistently recorded. This thorough, practical and evidence-based book provides guidance for professionals and parents caring for children and young people at risk of self-harm and suicide.

Claudine Fox and Keith Hawton discuss risk factors for self-harm, including depression, substance abuse and antisocial behaviour, and critically examine key screening instruments that can be used to assess risk. They describe how suicidal behaviour can be managed and prevented, and look at the effectiveness of aftercare treatment for those who self-harm, including school-based suicide-prevention programmes and family therapy. Also addressed are common myths about self-harm and the problem of varying definitions in this field.

Deliberate Self-Harm in Adolescence clearly summarises and evaluates current research into suicidal behaviour – it is essential reading for social workers, mental health professionals, GPs, teachers and parents.

Claudine Fox is a Research Fellow at the Centre for Primary Health Care Studies, University of Warwick. Her other research interests include childhood onset eating problems and children's knowledge and understanding of mental as well as physical illness. **Keith Hawton** is Professor of Psychiatry and Director of the Centre for Suicide Research at Oxford University. He is co-editor of the *International Handbook of Suicide and Attempted Suicide* and has been presented with awards from the International Association for Suicide Prevention (1995), the American Association of Suicidology (2001) and the American Foundation for Suicide Prevention (2002).